CRIME SURVEYS AND VICTIMS OF CRIME

CRIME SURVEYS AND VICTIMS OF CRIME

LAURENCE KOFFMAN

Reader in Law, University of Sussex

UNIVERSITY OF WALES PRESS • CARDIFF • 1996

British Library Cataloguing in Publication Data

A catalogue record for this book is available from the British Library.

ISBN 0-7083-1364-7

Typeset at the University of Wales Press
Printed in England by Bookcraft, Midsomer Norton, Avon

This book is dedicated to the memory of my father

Contents

Preface

This book is intended primarily for the general reader with an interest in crime rates, victimization, and research into these areas. There are many useful books aimed at more specialized readers already in existence. However, there are relatively few works which concentrate on explaining the development and progress of crime survey research, and it is hoped that the book will also be of interest to students pursuing law, criminology, and other social science courses.

This project came about indirectly as a result of my experience teaching criminal justice courses to law students. When looking at crime rates and victim surveys with these students, I used to comment on the paucity of research into rural crime and victimization. I decided to try to do something about this by conducting a victim survey in the Aberystwyth area. Although there was widespread support for such an initiative, it proved difficult to attract sufficient funding for a large-scale survey. Fortunately, I received financial support from the Sir David Hughes Parry Fund, the Society of Public Teachers of Law, Manweb, the Centre for Law in Rural Areas, and the University of Wales, Aberystwyth. The generosity of these bodies enabled me to undertake a small-scale victim survey, using professional interviewers, which is described in chapter 5.

I have been fortunate to receive help and advice from a number of people, both when planning the Aberystwyth crime survey and also during the writing of this book. In particular, I owe a debt of gratitude to the late Jane Morgan who was so enthusiastic about the Aberystwyth project before her untimely death in 1992. I benefited greatly from discussions with Jane on victimization research, and our intention was for the Aberystwyth survey to be a collaborative project. Sadly, this was not possible; she is greatly missed by all who knew her and worked with her.

I wish to thank Ken Pease for his invaluable advice and encouragement on a wide range of matters and for his generosity with his time. I am also very grateful to Pat Mayhew for her advice on victim research methodology, especially in relation to the British Crime Survey programme. Furthermore, I would like to acknowledge the support and advice of ex-colleagues in the Law Department at the University of Wales, Aberystwyth. In particular, I wish to thank Lillian Stevenson and Meirion Derrick and the staff of the Hugh Owen library for their help. Christine Davies typed most of the manuscript at Aberystwyth and Louise Tilley typed the later revisions and amendments at Sussex University. I wish to record my thanks to both of them for their word-processing skills and for their good natured assistance. I am also grateful to Liz Powell at the University of Wales Press for her work during the editing and production of this book. Lastly, but most importantly, I wish to thank my wife, Valerie, and daughter, Angela, for their constant support and encouragement throughout this and other projects.

The manuscript was completed in July 1995, but it has been possible to incorporate some more recent material into the final version of the book.

Laurence Koffman

1

Criminal Statistics

Introduction

The Criminal Statistics for England and Wales are published annually, with regular 'bulletin' reports in between, and purport to represent the incidence of criminal behaviour on a national scale. These figures are compiled by putting together the offences recorded by the police in each of the forty-three police areas in England and Wales. In drawing conclusions from these annual figures, there are pitfalls for the unwary, and opportunities for the unscrupulous. Inevitably, these 'official' or police statistics are an undercount of the crime which actually occurs, as they are no more than a reflection of the crimes actually reported to, and recorded by, the police. These figures tell us about those crimes which the public think are sufficiently serious to report, and which the police think are serious enough to record. Crimes which are neither reported nor recorded form the so-called 'dark figure' (i.e. the unknown quantity) of crime. Accordingly, an increase in public willingness to report crime, or a change in recording practices, can give an appearance of change in the crime rate which may not truly reflect the incidence of criminal behaviour.

There is no harm in the use of official criminal statistics as an indicator of the work done by the police, or even as a very rough measure of crime for allocating resources. But, unfortunately, the publication of the Criminal Statistics for England and Wales each year tends to give rise to misleading claims about the national crime rate, and to the drawing of frequently erroneous conclusions. There is evidence that over the last decade, for example, the considerable increase in recorded crime is partly due to changing trends in the reporting of crime by the public[1] and to changes in police recording practices. Victims of crime may be more inclined to report offences for a variety of reasons. Clearly, the seriousness of the incident will be a major determinant, in many cases, of the decision to report, and so it could be argued that increased reporting reflects a growth in more serious crime. But, even here, caution is required before accepting this argument. There is evidence that an increasing number of victims of theft and damage offences are today covered by insurance, and this could account for a larger proportion of victims (than ten years ago) reporting such incidents to the police.[2]

There may be other reasons for the greater willingness of victims to report offences. The last decade has seen an increase in the proportion of households which are owned or being bought by the occupier, and an owner-occupier is more likely to insure his or her home and its contents. An insured victim is more likely to report an offence against his or her property. Changes in the age structure of the general population may also lead to higher reporting rates, as older people appear more willing to report offences to the police. Easier access to a telephone may also encourage people to report offences to the police, but Skogan found little evidence to support this theory in his recent study of factors influencing the decision to report crimes to the police.[3] Overall, there can be little doubt that more offences which were previously thought to be in the 'not-so-serious' category are now being reported by victims for a variety of reasons.

The preceding discussion is not to suggest that crime is not on the increase; it is simply to explain that the growth of crime is not occurring at the rate expounded in the police statistics. Official figures have shown a dramatic rise in the second half of the twentieth century. It was estimated that recorded crime increased fivefold between 1945 and the early 1980s,[4] and since the mid-1980s the official crime rate has risen sharply. In some years, police statistics show a fall in recorded crime, but these figures must be treated with extreme caution for the reasons already stated. For example, between July 1993 and June 1994, there was a 5.5 per cent fall in recorded crime, which represented one of the largest decreases over the past forty years. But, during this twelve-month period, the recorded rate of violent crime rose by 6 per cent, despite the fall in many property offences, notably burglary, theft and vehicle crime. This overall decrease followed five years during which the official crime rate had risen at a considerable rate. It may also be the case that there has been a sudden drop in the reporting of less serious property crimes. It is certainly true that many victims either cannot afford insurance or, if they can afford it, may not claim if they have to pay the first part of any claim themselves.

It should be clear then that statements about the increase or decrease in crime, when based on police statistics, cannot be taken at face value. Since the early 1980s more reliable estimates of the crime rate for selective, but commonly occurring, offences have been provided by national and local crime surveys. These surveys will be described in detail later, but before this is done, it is instructive to look more closely at the problems involved in interpreting official crime figures.

The Use and Abuse of Recorded Crime Statistics

It is the recorded or police statistics which tend to form the basis of official statements about crime, or about 'law and order' policy and initiatives. Sometimes, speculative links are suggested between the crime rate and other areas of criminal justice policy. For example, it is occasionally claimed that the use of harsher penalties by the courts might have a significant deterrent effect on would be offenders and thus help to reduce the incidence of crime. There is little evidence to support such claims and, as the prison population for England and Wales is one of the highest in Western Europe, it is difficult to accept the argument that English courts are 'soft' on criminals. It is also unwise to see the recorded crime rate as an indicator of police efficiency. The recent decrease in officially recorded crime has not been accompanied by any appreciable improvement in the clear-up rate of recorded crime (which remains below 30 per cent). The crime rate may well be affected, however, by other police initiatives, such as crime prevention programmes, public information and the targeting of certain strategic offences. It should not be thought that nothing can be done about the crime rate, or that crime must inexorably rise each year, but we must be wary of false claims and simplistic solutions that have little or no bearing on the incidence of crime.

The first area of caution, as noted above, is in relation to the statistics on which official pronouncements and policy are based. To appreciate fully the shortcomings of official figures, it is important to understand the processes and decisions on which they are based. The first point to note is that they are not an objective measurement of crime, but rather, they are a reflection of a complex reaction to crime by the public and by the police. In other words, the official figures represent the social response to crime and it is a response which does not remain constant over time. For example, a heightened public awareness of a social problem, such as drug misuse amongst the young, may lead to increased reporting and greater police vigilance. This collective response will thus be reflected in the official crime rate whether or not the behaviour in question has become more common. Let us consider more closely the reaction to crime and how this shapes the recorded crime rate.

The processing and counting of crime reflects both the public response to it and the police's own administrative procedures and priorities. The police are heavily dependent on the public to bring crime to their attention. Estimates vary, but research suggests that in around 80–90 per cent (or more) of cases the police rely on the public to bring offences to their attention.[5] For this reason, we should start by considering why a crime might go unreported. Much depends on the perception of what is and what is not crime.

Many offences are of a 'victimless' nature, particularly those offences concerned with public morality, such as prostitution-related crime, non-addictive drug use and the provision of other illicit materials and services. Participants are unlikely to regard themselves as victims and complaints are likely to be made only where such conduct becomes a public nuisance (e.g., soliciting in residential areas). In other cases, such as shop-lifting offences, the 'victim' might be a company or business rather than an individual. The victim here may be unaware of the offence, or if aware, may decide not to report it. For example, computer fraud might not be reported by companies so as not to destroy public confidence. Non-reporting is particularly important in relation to crimes committed by employees, i.e. 'workplace' crime. Although such estimates must be treated with caution, it has been stated that thefts from work cost around £3 billion each year,[6] but this is hardly reflected in the official crime statistics because of the low reporting rate of such crime.[7]

The status of the victim may be a crucial determinant of whether an offence will be reported. Although procedures are improving (with the setting up of 'helplines' for instance), many thousands of crimes committed against children each year are not incorporated in the official crime figures. Children may suffer sexual abuse or assault at home, or may be victims of physical or psychological intimidation at school (i.e. 'bullying'). They may also be victims of crimes committed against the household in which they live, suffering shock and distress.[8] Other acts of violence committed in the home may well go unreported. Female victims of so-called 'domestic' violence may choose not to report incidents for a variety of reasons: they may fear reprisals and further violence from their attacker; they may feel embarrassed or in some way to blame; they may wish to avoid splitting up their family; or they may believe that the police will not be interested in the crime. In view of the publicity given to recent police initiatives aimed at improving their response to 'domestic' violence, an increase in reporting of this crime might be expected. (Domestic Violence Units have been set up in many police areas, together with 'at risk' registers and a more sympathetic approach to victims. These measures were reinforced in 1990 by John Patten, then a Home Office minister, who stated that 'brutality in the home is just as much a crime as any other sort of violence'.)

A common reason for not reporting an incident to the police is that the victim considers the offence too minor, or that it involves no direct loss. In the most recent 'sweep' of the British Crime Survey[9] this was the most frequent reason, given by 55 per cent of victims, for not reporting offences. Similar results were obtained from a recent mid-Wales crime survey which is discussed in chapter 5. However, a victim's perception of offence seriousness can be influenced by a variety of factors. We have noted earlier that the possibility of an insurance claim may well be influential in a decision to report what might otherwise be regarded as a trivial incident. The victim's assessment of the likely police response may also determine whether or not to report. Another factor might be whether the offender is known personally to the victim – as we saw in relation to 'domestic' violence – with the victim being reluctant to involve the police despite the seriousness of the incident.

Some very serious offences go unreported for a mixture of psychological and practical reasons, and even because of a profound distrust of the resulting criminal justice process in dealing with the complaint and the offender. The offence of rape is a good example of how a number of (often interrelated) reasons may inhibit the rate of reporting by victims. Indeed, some researchers argue that no more than one third of all rapes are reported; some put this figure even lower.[10] Care must also be taken not to assess offence seriousness purely in terms of the value of property either stolen or damaged. Many victims of crime, and many who suffer multiple victimization, are amongst the poorest members of society and can least afford to replace or repair their property. The theft of, say, £50 may be insignificant to a wealthy person, but may be devastating to someone living in impoverished circumstances. For example, in the mid-1980s the Merseyside Crime Survey found that multiple victimization was much more common amongst inner city residents than for the more wealthy suburban dwellers. When asked about the impact of the offence upon them, one third of victims living in the poorest areas assessed it as 'very big', in contrast with only one tenth of wealthier victims.[11]

So far we have considered some of the reasons why an offence may not be reported to the police. But not all offences which *are* reported to them are recorded as such by the police. For instance, the police may not agree with the victim's perception of an incident and may decide that either no crime has been committed, or that it is a crime of less seriousness than the victim's report suggested. If the incident is particularly trivial, the police may feel that it is not worth their time and the paperwork involved in formally recording it. This may be acceptable so long as it is based on a genuine evaluation of the incident and its effect on the victim. But if the police response simply reflects their own priorities, not based on any public discussion or agreement, then such decisions may cause ill-feeling and undermine public confidence. If the police fail to follow up, or even record, offences below a certain seriousness threshold, the public will cease to report such incidents (and possibly more serious ones) to them.

The recording rate of crime by the police reflects a number of operational, administrative and legal factors. For example, the decision to 'screen-out' certain less serious offences of vandalism and burglary has been referred to above. In the late 1980s, the Metropolitan Police introduced (and soon abandoned) a points system to indicate which burglaries would be followed up based on the potential 'solvability' of the offence. This was a much criticized policy which obviously had an effect on the rate of both crime reporting and recording. The fact that it reflected police priorities and bureaucracy and remained unchallengeable by the public served to emphasize the controversial nature of this scheme. We have also noted (above) the changing police response to domestic violence. In 1990, every police area was issued with guidelines about setting up registers for victims 'at risk' of domestic assault. This scheme was based on a new approach to such incidents by West Yorkshire police, whose Chief Constable stated in 1988 that 'all officers should act to enforce the law when an assault takes place within the domestic environment in exactly the same way that they would act in the case of an attack by a stranger or in respect of any assault outside the home'.[12]

As part of a package of measures designed to ensure that domestic violence is taken more seriously by the police (in response to widespread criticism of previous inaction), these 'at risk' registers enable information about victims to be compiled and acted upon, as the information is of use to specially trained officers working in the domestic violence units. This is not the appropriate place for an evaluation of this initiative, but it should be noted that there are drawbacks involved in setting up specialist units, such as marginalizing the problem rather than making all officers aware of it. But one possible result of this change in policy by the police is that the number of recorded incidents will increase considerably.[13]

A good example of this phenomenon occurred after the passing of the Children and Young Persons Act 1969, which aimed to introduce *inter alia*, a 'treatment' philosophy for dealing with young offenders. As part of this new approach, most police forces established juvenile bureaux in which juvenile cautions were recorded formally, whereas in the past no formal record may have been made of an incident. Due to this enhancement of police efficiency in recording incidents involving juvenile offenders, it appeared that juvenile crime increased sharply after the enactment of the 1969 legislation. The unwary were soon blaming the perceived leniency of the Act for this turn of events, but it is more likely that a change in the police procedures for recording incidents was responsible for much of the change in the crime rate.

The first 'sweep' of the British Crime Survey in 1982 drew attention to the non-recording by the police of many crimes reported to them by the public. The researchers involved acknowledged that accurate estimates are difficult to make due to numerous sources of error. But, despite these problems, they compared the BCS findings with the official crime statistics and concluded that the police recorded as notifiable offences, about two-thirds of offences involving property loss or damage, and less than half of the violent incidents, which were reported to them.[14] Moreover, it was estimated (tentatively) that the police recorded only around 70 per cent of burglaries reported to them by victims and the public.

It should also be noted that police recording practices may vary from one area to another. For example, two geographical areas may have a similar crime rate and similar number of offences reported to the police by the public. But if these reported incidents are processed differently by the police in these two hypothetical areas, then the resulting official statistics will present one area as having a more serious crime problem than the other. It was pointed out in the first British Crime Survey report[15] that the Nottingham police area appeared consistently, at that time, to be the most crime-ridden area of the country in relation to its size of population. The researchers thought that this was unlikely to reflect the actual rate of crime throughout the country, but more probably was an indication of crime reporting patterns and the likelihood that Nottingham police record a higher proportion of crimes which are brought to their attention by the public. (For research contrasting the recording rates by different police districts in London, see R. Sparks et al.).[16] In an earlier piece of research, McCabe and Sutcliffe compared the recording practices of the Oxford and Salford police.[17] Once again, different rates of recording by the two police forces were found by the researchers, with Oxford having the lower recording rate.

Many studies of police discretion and police handling of reported incidents suggest that allegations of assault are frequently not recorded as offences by the police. The police might argue that many of these incidents are 'domestic' in nature (see earlier discussion of this), or that the alleged offender was related to or known to the victim, and that such complaints are frequently withdrawn. Sometimes it will be officially recorded that a complaint was withdrawn by the victim, and the police may use such instances to support their claim that this type of alleged incident is frequently a waste of their time. However, it is equally possible that, in many cases, a complaint is recorded as withdrawn because the victim believes that the police are not prepared to do anything and therefore sees no point in pursuing the matter further.[18]

A further problem in assessing recorded rates of crime stems from counting methods used by the police in relation to a series of offences committed on one occasion, or where the offence involves a number of victims, or where the same offence is repeated over a long period of time. Since the early 1980s there have been stricter and more consistent rules, for the counting of notifiable offences, which are aimed at reducing the amount of discretion exercised by the police when recording crime in their area. However, it is virtually impossible to prevent some discrepancies in counting practices between police officers in different areas. Further differences may arise in relation to the recording of offences 'taken into consideration', and also in respect of offences admitted to the police by suspected and apprehended persons.[19] The Home Office has issued guidelines recently for the recording of burglaries after the Inspectorate of Constabulary, in 1994, found anomalies and different recording practices across seven divisions in the North West London Metropolitan Police area.

From this brief review of official, or recorded, crime statistics it should be evident that pronouncements about crime based on these figures alone must be treated with circumspection. As a starting point for the discussion of the incidence of crime, official statistics have their uses, particularly when augmented by the now ample evidence from crime and victim surveys. As a rough and ready guide for the allocation of resources and the planning of priorities, official statistics on crime can also be of some use. However, it is clear that these figures are a better indication of the public's response to crime and the police's attitudes to, and assumptions about, what is worth recording. Bentham, writing over 200 years ago, first referred to such statistics as a 'political barometer' enabling the well-being (or otherwise) of the nation to be observed and measured. But, in the words of Jones and Young, 'it has always been a barometer in which the glass is darkened, the mercury stuck and nobody agrees on how many times to shake it.'[20]

Crime Statistics: Some Recent Trends

We have seen how official crime statistics can mislead as well as inform about patterns of crime. Before going on to consider how a more accurate picture can be obtained from local and national crime surveys, it is interesting to look at recent reports, statistical bulletins, and pronouncements by ministers and others about crime. It is not intended to provide a comprehensive review of all recent reports and statements, but just a sample of them. The purpose of this brief review is to illustrate the bewildering mass of data which is presented to us all and the difficulties involved in interpreting this information.

Is crime on the increase or not? Notifiable offences (i.e. the more serious ones) recorded by the police fell by 5.5 per cent in the year to

July 1994, with 5.4 million offences recorded in the twelve-month period. Burglaries were down by 107,000 to 1.3 million, with theft and handling offences falling by 220,000 to 2.6 million. However, thefts from the person rose by 17 per cent, robberies increased by 5 per cent, and rapes increased by 15 per cent. It is worth noting that the fall in recorded crime in 1994 – and again in 1995 – is in stark contrast to the picture presented in the official figures for the years preceding this period. In the year ending June 1993, notifiable offences increased by 3.8 per cent to a total figure of 5.7 million. Even in respect of these figures, government ministers claimed a degree of success in so far as this was a slower rate of growth in crime than in the previous four years.[21] In the early 1990s, increases in the official crime figures were running at record levels, so the modest decrease in the last two years must be seen in this context. (After recorded crime dropped by 5 per cent in 1988, there followed a four-year period in which recorded crime rose by about 40 per cent.)

In relation to particular offences, the increase in recorded rape offences is worth noting. The increase of 15 per cent in the year to July 1994 continues the upward trend for this offence. The recorded figures have more than trebled in just over ten years.[22] Sexual offences and indecent assaults also increased during 1994. But, despite the alarming increase in the official statistics, it is very difficult to ascertain whether more women are now being attacked and raped, or whether more of those who are victims of such crimes are now coming forward and reporting the incident to the police. It is well established from research studies that only a small proportion of rape victims actually report the offence, so it would need only a modest upturn in reporting to give the impression of a large increase in the incidence of this crime. Women victims may be more willing to report attacks for a variety of reasons, and the police claim that publicity given to their improved handling of complaints and their treatment of victims has encouraged more rape victims to come forward.

Is crime a larger social problem in Britain than in other countries? It is certainly perceived as one of the most pressing social problems by respondents in crime surveys: for example, it was seen as the third largest social problem by respondents in the Merseyside Crime Survey, and as second only to unemployment as the most serious social problem facing residents on the poorest housing estates.[23] The extent of the crime problem cannot be measured by comparing the prison populations of different countries, as the rate of imprisonment is a reflection, *inter alia*, of sentencing practices of the courts. In the past, some countries have managed to reduce their prison populations at the same time that crime has been on the increase. The use of other strategies for diverting offenders from prosecution and from incarceration are possibly a more crucial determinant of the prison population than the rate of offending.[24]

Although cross-national or 'comparative' studies of crime and criminal justice systems are of great value to criminologists, most researchers are in agreement that official statistics of crime and punishment need treating with caution.[25] This does not prevent the widespread reporting of comparative statistical information on crime. For example, a recent article proclaimed that 'people are more likely to have their car stolen or their house burgled in Britain than in the United States',[26] quoting Professor Norval Morris's interpretation of international crime surveys. But much depends on which offences are being discussed, and it has also been claimed (based on Home Office figures released on 28 April 1993) that a person's chances of being assaulted are lower in Britain than in Norway, Spain, Germany, Finland, Holland, Canada, Australia and New Zealand.[27] The purpose of citing these statistics is to underline the difficulties in describing one country as having a bigger crime problem than another. Obviously, the relative size of population has to be taken into account, as does the interrelationship of certain types of offence, and the methods used in each country for both counting and recording offences.[28]

Sometimes recorded crime statistics are presented so as to show regional variations and crime patterns. We have been told recently, for example, that the overall rise in crime since 1991 has been greater outside the inner cities. In 1993, it was stated that recorded crime was rising at an annual rate of more than 10 per cent in a number of rural areas, which include Avon and Somerset, Cambridgeshire, Cheshire, Devon and Cornwall, and Staffordshire. In contrast, the crime rate was falling in the more densely populated areas of London, Liverpool and Newcastle.[29] The recorded crime figures for the forty-three police areas showed average increases of around 6 per cent in rural areas compared with a 1 per cent average increase in city areas. The changing patterns of crime, in regional terms, are sometimes expressed in 'league tables' of risk. In 1993, it was reported that certain traditionally high-crime areas had been overtaken by some areas which were once thought to be less crime-ridden. Table 1.1 is based on a House of Commons computer analysis of crime statistics which related crimes of violence to population.[30]

In addition to matching the number of offences of violence to the number of people in each police area, the House of Commons researchers also matched the number of vehicle-related offences to the number of cars, and the number of burglaries to the number of households in each area. In order to show the changing regional crime patterns, the researchers contrasted the present recorded crime figures with those found in 1979. It was claimed that the nationwide risk of

Table 1.1   **Crimes against the person: to June 1993**

	(1979 ranking)	Police authority	Offences per 100,000	Increase 1979–93 %
1	(1)	Nottinghamshire	997	91.2
2	(4)	London (inc.City)	961	180.5
3	(2)	Humberside	707	77.8
4	(8)	West Midlands	696	125.1
5	(6)	Merseyside	694	106.1
6	(7)	West Yorkshire	659	103.0
7	(16)	Greater Manchester	640	153.3
8	(9)	Gwent	623	104.3
9	(5)	Staffordshire	596	74.1
10	(21)	Leicestershire	577	165.6
11	(12)	Northumbria	570	97.7
12	(3)	Bedfordshire	561	51.7
13	(14)	Northamptonshire	555	109.4
14	(25)	Wiltshire	550	166.4
15	(37)	Dyfed-Powys	542	203.8
16	(10)	Cleveland	527	74.3
17	(13)	Derbyshire	524	95.2
18	(28)	Avon & Somerset	520	160.6
19	(19)	Cambridgeshire	516	125.6
20	(18)	S. Wales	515	117.8
21	(15)	Durham	500	93.6
22	(11)	S. Yorkshire	493	67.6
23	(35)	Kent	491	171.6
24	(31)	Cumbria	486	151.3
25	(20)	Lincolnshire	474	110.0
26	(17)	N. Wales	460	85.5
27	(22)	Hampshire	413	92.5
28	(42)	Gloucestershire	411	176.9
29	(29)	Suffolk	410	108.3
30	(35)	Cheshire	378	96.2
31	(23)	W. Mercia	374	75.0
32	(32)	Devon & Cornwall	360	86.4
33	(26)	Essex	359	75.2
34	(39)	Warwickshire	356	116.9
35	(40)	Norfolk	329	112.0
36	(41)	Dorset	324	110.3
37	(36)	Thames Valley	319	78.4
38	(24)	Sussex	317	52.8
39	(38)	N. Yorkshire	310	74.1
40	(30)	Lancashire	295	52.1
41	(27)	Surrey	289	44.0
42	(34)	Hertfordshire	281	46.2

burglary per household has more than doubled in this fourteen-year period, with West Yorkshire having the highest rate and Dyfed-Powys the lowest. It was claimed that, in 1979, the risk of burglary was five times greater on Merseyside than in Gloucestershire, and four times that in Avon and Somerset; but in 1993, households in Gloucestershire and Avon and Somerset now faced a greater risk of burglary than those on Merseyside.[31]

It is worth underlining the point that crime statistics can be used and presented in a variety of ways and for a number of purposes. In the case of the figures just cited, the purpose of the analysis was to embarrass the government with the extent of the growth in crime since the Conservative Party came to power under Mrs Thatcher in 1979. Furthermore, the statistics were used to rebut the statement by John Major that crime was predominantly an urban problem, by showing a large increase in risk of crime (especially violent crime) in more rural county areas.[32] It might be questioned why the crime rate should be seen as a party political issue, but with the Conservatives having pledged themselves from the outset to a 'law and order' policy, the opposition wished to link the crime rate directly to government policies and to suggest that, even in its traditional strongholds, the government was failing in its fight against crime.

To put the matter bluntly, crime is now a central political issue with the major political parties attempting to score points off one another and with each claiming that their own policies are more conducive to tackling crime than those of their rivals. In explaining the growth in crime one is similarly faced with a bewildering mass of theories and statistical associations and the choice of one theory over another can often reflect the political standpoint of the commentator. For example, those on the political right might attribute crime, *inter alia*, to declining moral standards, lack of parental control and discipline, lenient sentencing, and the harmful effects of television and popular culture. Those on the political left might be more willing to see the rise in crime as a reflection of the discrepancies in wealth and opportunity that exist in our society. Even here there is a paradox, for the crime rate reflects opportunity to a considerable extent – the advent of the motor car as a widely owned item of property has led to a vast increase in crime – which would seem to link crime to growing prosperity rather than recession.

The present government has resisted, for many years, any suggestion that crime is linked to unemployment or recession. But recent studies make this view less tenable, as it appears that the rise in unemployment amongst young men and the growth in burglary at the same time are closely connected.[33] Another research finding unpopular with the government is that youth work schemes and projects might be capable of preventing crime by young people. (This was explored in a survey by management consultants Coopers and Lybrand for the Prince's Trust.) The report, published in 1994, is a cost-benefit analysis of youth work in preventing juvenile crime, which estimates that youth crime in Britain costs more than £7 billion a year, whereas youth projects cost only £240 a year per teenager. The government, however, remains to be convinced of the efficacy of such programmes and it has stated that official evaluation of youth work schemes will not be completed until at least 1996. Many commentators have pointed out the irony that the government is willing to commit large sums of money to custodial institutions for young offenders despite the fact that there is little evidence of their effectiveness.[34]

In contrast to the general perception of increasing lawlessness amongst the young, a recent analysis by the Central Statistical Office[35] suggests that the number of children (aged 10–16) found guilty or cautioned for all types of offence in England and Wales fell by more than a third between 1981 and 1992. These figures present a different picture of child crime from that found in many parts of the mass media, and in the more florid speeches of some politicians on the 'right', where blame is placed upon single parents, working mothers, absenteeism from school, and 'do-gooders' in the criminal justice system for the supposed increase in child offending. But, again, we must be wary of taking these crude figures at face value.[36] To make any genuine comparison of crime rates during this period it would be necessary to look at population changes and the number of children in this age group, as is acknowledged in the Central Statistical Office's report. Changes in policy may also be instrumental in bringing about the drop in convictions and official cautions among the young. If the police have adopted a policy of informal warnings and unrecorded cautions, then this may well account (at least, in part) for the apparent decrease in crime. Also, these statistics are dealing with known or 'official' crime. Further evidence would be needed from victim and self-report studies to gain some insight into the 'dark figure' of crime.

Thus crime figures and research findings are not received by an objective and apolitical audience. Rather, they are used in a way which best suits the purpose of the user: for example, to embarrass a government, or to attack the supposed leniency of the courts or the perceived inefficiency of the police. A related problem is that the government has some influence over the funding and dissemination of crime research. The Home Office Research and Planning Unit which is responsible each year for a number of excellent (but expensive) research reports has recently denied that some of its studies have been delayed in publication. But a recent newspaper report[37] gave details of a Home Office research study for which no publication date had been set. This research involved an international study of youth and crime, interviewing young people in thirteen Western countries, and was co-ordinated by the Dutch Ministry of Justice. In addition, there were five national studies based on Holland, England and Wales, Spain, Portugal and Switzerland. Although the Home Office carried out the English study, the findings were obtained by the *Guardian* newspaper from the Dutch Ministry of Justice. The alleged tardiness on the part of the Home Office in making these research findings public has fuelled speculation that ministers are 'shelving' or delaying research projects which are inconsistent with government policy, especially in relation to its 'tough' approach on law and order. According to the Dutch report of this international research on youth crime, England has an appreciably lower rate of violent crime amongst young people aged 14–21 than the other four countries which were studied in depth. The rate of vandalism was especially low in comparison to the other four. The research also suggests that, in contrast to official police statistics in England and Wales, there was either no difference, or lower offending rates, for ethnic minorities when compared with white youths in relation to property or violent crime.[38]

Just as crime figures can be used or misrepresented to comment on social trends and policies, so too can figures about the clear-up rate of crime. It is sometimes suggested that such statistics can be seen as an indicator of police efficiency, but it should be remembered that the number of offences cleared up depends, *inter alia*, on police recording practices, the type of offences committed, admissions by suspected persons, and offences taken into consideration by the courts. For example, a police officer may be more willing to 'no-crime' an incident if he or she feels that the offence is unlikely to be cleared up by someone being charged or cautioned for the crime. It could also be argued that lower clear-up rates might be more a reflection of the increased willingness of the public to report crime than any decline in police performance.[39] Although clear-up statistics must be treated with the same caution as most other crime statistics, it does seem that increasing police manpower and resources is not the simple answer to falling clear-up rates.[40] Indeed, it has been shown that the Metropolitan Police area achieved little improvement in its clear-up rate between 1976 and 1981 in spite of a 12 per cent increase in manpower.[41]

The most recent figures paint a depressing picture of the rate of crimes cleared up by the police. According to Home Office statistics, the overall clear-up rate (as a percentage of recorded crime) fell steadily from 36 per cent in 1980 to 31 in 1989, but in 1992, it dropped to just 25 per cent. In a recent survey,[42] based on information obtained from thirty-nine police areas in England and Wales, it was revealed that this decrease continued in 1993.[43] A decline in the number of crimes cleared up, in relation to the number of crimes recorded, was reported by twenty-two of the thirty-nine areas for which figures were available. A particularly dramatic example is that of Cheshire, where the clear-up rate has dropped from 50 per cent in 1990 to 26 in 1993. But, as stated earlier, there may be a number of reasons behind such a change and it cannot be seen as a reliable yardstick of police efficiency and performance. Some crimes, such as burglary and theft from vehicles, have a much lower clear-up rate than others, such as sexual offences and violence against the person. So the clear-up rate in an area might reflect changing crime patterns, changing trends in the reporting of crime, as well as in the recording of these incidents. It may also be related to methods used by the police to clear up crimes, such as discontinuing the practice of interviewing prisoners serving custodial sentences in the hope of clearing up unsolved offences.

Conclusion

The purpose of this brief review of recent statistical information about crime and its presentation by researchers, the media and politicians, is to illustrate the difficulty in drawing any firm conclusions on the subject. If approached with caution, the figures we have looked at can be of considerable value in understanding (or at least observing) trends, allocating resources, and developing strategies for responding to crime. But the statistics can conceal as much as they reveal. They may, for example, be presented in a certain way (or even suppressed) for political purposes. The interpretation of the figures, especially in relation to determining the causes of criminal behaviour, will vary according to the political tastes and opinions of the commentator. Much of this is to state the obvious, but it should be clearly acknowledged in any discussion of criminal statistics. Of course, there is a need for reliable criminological research and the publication of statistics on crime; without this, an informed public debate on the subject would not be possible. But the tendentious nature of much of the public comment on the subject should be noted.

2

Victims and the Criminal Justice System

Before looking in detail at victimization research, it is worth pausing to consider why the study of victims and the interest in victims' rights has today assumed such importance to academics, practitioners, politicians and many other groups. What are the factors which have led to victimology becoming a central part of modern criminology and criminal justice studies? There is, of course, no simple answer to this question. Instead, a number of possible reasons can be offered to explain this burgeoning interest in victims at all stages of the criminal justice process. One approach is to look at some of the traditional concerns of criminology and penology and to recognize the growing importance of studying victims and victims' rights. There are also political considerations behind some of the developments, and these too need to be acknowledged. What follows is not an exhaustive list of reasons for the development of interest in victims; it is merely an overview of *some* of the principal ideas behind this development.

A student embarking on the study of criminology today will expect to find the study of victims and the incidence of victimization as central concerns of the subject, and will not be disappointed. But, perhaps surprisingly, until the last two decades or so there was relatively little (if any) interest shown in victims and victimology by most researchers. Traditional criminology focused predominantly on the offender, not the victim, and was concerned with the ætiology of crime and not victimization.[1] This tradition is illustrated by the work of researchers who studied the shape and formation of criminals' skulls in the hope of detecting distinguishing characteristics, and by the work of Lombroso, who attempted to identify a distinct biological 'criminal' type, and also by other theorists who tried to establish the genetic, or psychological differences between criminals and 'normal' people. Many of these early studies were conducted on prisoners and groups of offenders and they failed to treat the definition of 'crime' or the notion of 'criminality' as problematic. They hoped that the study of what made the criminal different from law-abiding citizens might also lead to finding ways of 'curing' or treating this criminality. For criminal behaviour tended to be depicted as a disease or illness – which was why a great deal of criminological research was concerned with finding its roots or causes. Much of this type of research was carried out by scientists and many of the theories which were put forward to explain the distinctive characteristics of offenders reflected the prevailing or avant-garde theories of their respective disciplines. So when early positivist theories of a biological nature gave way to psychological or psychiatric theorizing about crime, it was not surprising that the writings of Freud were briefly influential and, later, the conditioning theories of writers such as Eysenck.[2] Even the emerging academic discipline of sociology, which showed great interest in the study of crime, initially made little difference to the general orientation of traditional criminology.

The 1960s, however, witnessed an important refocusing of sociological research into crime, and, more particularly, 'deviance' (which became a central concept). This new approach to crime was less 'scientific', if judged in terms of its use of the scientific method. What this movement did achieve was to challenge the ideas about criminality as some objectively defined concept and to point out the need to study the social construction of crime and deviance. The early development of this new 'labelling' (or social reaction) perspective is very much associated with American sociologists, such as Howard Becker,[3] Edwin Lemert, Kai Erikson and John Kitsuse. Becker stated, for example,

> What laymen want to know about deviants is: why do they do it? How can we account for their rule-breaking? What is there about them that leads them to do forbidden things? Scientific research has tried to find answers to these questions. In doing so it has accepted the common-sense premise that there is something inherently deviant (qualitatively distinct) about acts that break (or seem to break) social rules. It has also accepted the common-sense assumption that the deviant act occurs because some characteristic of the person who commits it makes it necessary or inevitable that he should. Scientists do not ordinarily question the label 'deviant' when it is applied to particular acts or people but rather take it as given. In so doing, they accept the values of the group making the judgment.[4]

This perspective was soon embraced by many sociologists in Britain, although not all writers followed exactly the same approach to the study of deviance.[5] Rather belatedly, the concepts of crime and deviance were treated as problematic. The concern was no longer simply with the deviant 'actor', but with those who judged the conduct to be deviant and the process by which they arrived at this conclusion. This new perspective looked at the social reaction to certain forms of behaviour, by observations and other qualitative methods, and asked why certain acts are labelled as criminal (or deviant) whilst others, which may be equally harmful, are not. For example, what is the difference between the youthful 'exuberance' (or 'pranks') of university students or local rugby players, and the vandalism or rowdiness of working-class youths on inner-city streets? Why is taking items from work by employees or office staff seen by many as acceptable (or at least defensible), whilst taking money from a till is seen as theft?[6]

In short, society has certain preconceived views about the 'stereotype' of the criminal, and those people who do not fit this stereotype, however harmful their behaviour may be, may escape the label of criminal or deviant actor. For example, everyone agrees that an assault on a woman, or an indecent assault on a child, when committed by strangers are very serious offences requiring the full weight of the law to be invoked. Yet views about violence or sexual abuse in the home have often, in the past, been more equivocal. Many people found it difficult to accept that their respectable (seeming) middle-class neighbour frequently assaults his wife or children. The law enforcement process was also (and still is) very slow to react, preferring to redefine such acts as 'domestic' incidents and to rationalize why it was difficult to apply the law to such situations. It is a serious indictment of our criminal justice system that, whilst room can always be found in our overcrowded prisons to accommodate the recidivist property offender, many violent men escape censure (let alone punishment) so long as their victim is a member of their family. The victim's protection may lie, not in the law, but in the voluntary efforts of those who run refuges for female victims of 'domestic' violence. It required the efforts of individuals, rather than any official response by the criminal justice system, to establish even this very basic level of support and protection. Erin Pizzey founded the Chiswick Women's Aid in 1971 and, since then, many similar refuges have been set up.[7] But it should not be forgotten that female victims of this type of violence (and arguably other types too) are still poorly served by the criminal justice system.[8]

The revelation of this type of conduct showed the deficiencies of traditional criminology, which had sought to study the factors which distinguished the criminal from 'normal' law-abiding people. It now seemed that such a distinction was deeply flawed. Many apparently normal people were also criminal (or deviant) and what was now of interest was how society in general, or the law enforcement process in particular, dealt with their infractions. This 'labelling' or social reaction perspective was not a theory of criminal behaviour, nor did it seek to propose solutions to questions about the causes of crime. Its proponents 'wanted to enlarge the area taken into consideration in the study of deviant phenomena by including in it activities of others than the allegedly deviant actor.'[9] The interest in a 'labelling' approach revealed the absurdity of criminological theories of a pseudo-scientific nature which attempted to isolate criminogenic factors and succeeded (for the most part) in removing crime from its situational context and in ignoring the importance of considering social definitions of crime. Other writers also contributed to these developments. For example Edwin Sutherland carried out pioneering research in America into the 'white-collar' crimes of companies and high-status organizations.[10] There was also valuable work carried out in Britain of a similar nature; for example, W. G. Carson's study of the enforcement (and non-enforcement) of health and safety legislation in factories suggested that the differential enforcement of the law, by agencies entrusted with policing the legislation, was a potentially rewarding area of study for criminologists and sociologists of law.[11]

This type of sociological research represented a significant departure from positivist schools of criminology which focused narrowly on the individual criminal, failed to treat 'criminality' as problematic, and tended to overpredict the incidence of crime. It also led to further scepticism about the value of official criminal statistics, which record only certain types of crime and reflect particular forms of law enforcement.[12] The emphasis had thus shifted from measuring crime, and theorizing about its ætiology, to attempting to explain the processes by which certain forms of behaviour are labelled as criminal and how the law is enforced in relation to different types of misconduct. In this sense there was a movement away from the traditional use of crime statistics as part of criminological studies, and some have argued that there was a tendency to eschew quantitative methods and also to look down upon empiricism.[13] But the last two decades have witnessed yet another shift in emphasis, with a renaissance of empirical and statistical research which has been an important part of the developing study of victimology.

As we have seen, the labelling or social reaction perspective encouraged a wider view of criminology than the traditional approaches. The subject was no longer solely concerned with the characteristics of the offender, but was to include the societal reaction to misconduct and the processing of criminals. It could (at least potentially) also embrace the study of those who suffer the consequences of crime and how it affects them. So, to this extent, the labelling perspective prepared the way for the emerging discipline of victimology. But, in other respects, it was the shortcomings of the new perspective which stimulated an interest in victimology and a new empiricism. For example, despite the subjective response to a considerable amount of law-breaking, it could not be ignored that a large proportion of crimes are committed by a relatively small section of society. Moreover, the effects of this crime hit certain groups much more than others, both in terms of the frequency with which they are victimized and in the consequences of their victimization. It is the most vulnerable and (often) disadvantaged groups in inner cities which suffer the worst impact of crime. These groups also tend to suffer the harshest forms of law enforcement and social control. It is ironic that those who are stopped and searched by the police, for example, are also quite likely to be victims of crime than themselves.[14] This was an area of criminology ripe for exploration by means of both quantitative and qualitative research.

It could be argued that there is also a strong tendency towards the 'scientific' approach to criminology and that this is often seen as involving measurement and quantification. This tendency may be suppressed for short periods (as we have seen) but is never far from the surface. It is slightly ironic that much of the statistical analysis and measurement which used to characterize the study of criminals now seems to be directed towards the study of victims – with many of the same variables being closely analysed, such as age, gender, ethnic group, social class, employment status and so on. The early development of victimization research was concerned predominantly with measurement, and is sometimes referred to as 'administrative' criminology. Naturally, the findings of national 'crime' surveys (discussed in the next chapter) could inform crime prevention initiatives and other responses to crime, but they were not directly concerned with social justice and political reform. Once again, a detached, scientific perspective was adopted by these researchers who were largely government-funded, and their aim was to *describe*: that is, to develop more reliable methods of 'mapping' crime and victimization.

The British Crime Survey programme which began in the early 1980s is a good example of this development of the new criminology. This national victimization survey was rigorously designed and conducted, its findings were of considerable interest and were presented clearly in an objective manner. But this research was soon criticized for failing to show the particular vulnerability of certain groups such as women and ethnic minority groups. The British Crime Survey (BCS) refined its methodology and later included ethnic minority 'booster' samples, but it has not always been regarded as an effective method of surveying violent crime against women. The BCS was also criticized for 'playing down' the risks of victimization by presenting risks in terms of the statistically average person. It was pointed out by critics[15] that there is no such person and that, in reality, certain groups are far more frequently victimized (and repeatedly victimized) than others. By failing either to discover or to comment on this, it was argued, the findings of the national survey were flawed and potentially misleading.

Similar criticisms were also applied to the BCS findings on fear of crime. The researchers had suggested that levels of fear were alarmingly high in relation to certain groups who appeared to be rarely victimized. Once again, the critics retorted that fear (for example, amongst women) *was* realistic when a more sensitive measurement of victimization rates was carried out.[16] The 'new realist' wave of victimization researchers had a different sense of mission and used their findings in a different way. Regional or local crime surveys were funded largely by local councils and were more 'political' in the sense that they were motivated by a reformist agenda and a desire to expose the link between social disadvantage, vulnerability and victimization. The reports of these studies were not couched in the guarded, 'scientific' terms of the administrative criminologists, but rather they were overtly critical of political and social policy and, in particular, the law enforcement arrangements in urban areas.[17] The 'new realist' researchers have themselves been criticized for reading too much into their own data and for generally pushing the victimization survey methodology beyond the boundaries of its reliability – especially in drawing such firm conclusions from respondents' attitudes and opinions. These are matters to which we shall return in the following chapters. It is not necessary here to evaluate the criticisms of either the national or local crime survey research. All that is intended at this point is to chart the development of victimology within the broader discipline of criminology.[18] Of course, victimology is not based solely on victimization surveys, but such surveys have become an important tool of researchers working in this area. Moreover, it is a research method which is not without its critics.[19]

The development of victimology as a central component of the new realist criminology cannot be seen in isolation from the burgeoning political movement in support of victims' rights which is closely associated with the United States. Nor should it be divorced from other developments in the criminal justice system which have focused greater attention on victims and on compensation or reparation. These trends all require some consideration before we return to the subject of victimization research, for they help to explain the abundant interest in empirical research on victims.

How can one account for the growth in interest in the plight of victims? In the past, the victim appeared to be the forgotten person in the criminal justice system. Once a crime was reported and the police decided to investigate the offence and proceed against an offender (if caught), the victim's role was simply that of a witness at the trial. The victim had no say (and still has not) in the decision as to the appropriate charge(s) or the eventual sentence of an accused person found guilty at court. This is not surprising, as these decisions involve interests which are not solely concerned with the wishes of the victim. There may be technical legal reasons for preferring one charge (say, assault occasioning actual bodily harm) to another (such as inflicting grievous bodily harm). There may be other considerations when deciding on the appropriate punishment than merely satisfying the wishes of the victim or the victim's family. The sentencer will have to view the offender's conduct in the overall context of other cases dealt with by the court, in accordance with the offender's *mens rea* and culpability, and have regard to any statutory or common law guidance.[20] If the courts were to concentrate more on the harm done to the victim and less on the intention of the offender, sentencing principles would have to be altered accordingly to reflect this change of attitude.

This type of problem was well illustrated by the case of *Andrew Bray* (in March 1994) who was sentenced to five years' imprisonment for the manslaughter of Jonathon Roberts, a seventeen-year-old shop assistant who tried to apprehend Bray in the act of shoplifting. Bray claimed that the force he used was intended only in order to escape from Jonathon Roberts and that no serious harm to him was intended. Put simply, the criminal intention was not to commit a serious offence, but the resulting harm was very serious indeed. Should the law punish Bray according to his intention, or so as to reflect the harm he caused to the victim (and the victim's family)? One leading expert has commented that it is an important principle 'that the offender must be sentenced for the offence of which he has been convicted, not for an offence of which some people think he may be guilty but which cannot be proved' (i.e. murder), and that 'no sentence . . . will ever satisfy the conflicting expectations of the bereaved relatives for a sentence which properly recognises their loss, and of the defendant for a sentence which does not unfairly punish him for the unintended consequences of his action'.[21]

It is possible to concur with David Thomas's arguments in general terms whilst having some reservations about their application to this particular case; after all, Bray used violence to escape lawful apprehension by a younger person whilst in the course of committing another crime. It appears that the vulnerability of the victim in respect of his age and his attempt to prevent a crime (rather than ignoring it) were not relevant factors in sentencing the offender. But the general exclusion of the victim's (or the victim's family's) wishes from the sentencing process is obviously defensible, despite the pressure from some quarters to involve victims more in the sentencing or 'penal' stage of the criminal justice process. The interests and needs of victims are clearly relevant at all stages of the criminal justice system but, in Britain at least, there are limits to how far these interests can be allowed to outweigh other considerations.

In contrast, the development of victims' interests and rights in the United States has been more difficult to contain. Part of the impetus for this development was the desire to promote a more punitive response to offending, and the American victim movement has been characterized as rather reactionary in its sympathies.[22] The involvement of victims in the criminal justice system of the United States is more pervasive than in Britain. Even in relation to plea-bargaining and early-release decisions, some states involve victims by seeking their views. In addition, victims in many states have the opportunity to make 'statements' about the impact of the crime on them and about their opinion as to the desirable level of sentencing required.

In Britain, recognition of victims' rights has not been so politically oriented as in the United States and is not viewed as such a reactionary development. As we shall see, attention has centred on improving support and information for victims at all stages in the process, but particularly by the establishment of victim support schemes throughout the country.[23] There has also been a movement towards compensating the victims of certain types of crime at the sentencing stage. But before looking at some of these developments, it is worth considering why there has been this upsurge of interest in upholding the rights of victims.

There can be no doubt that the treatment of victims of crime was (and often still is) far from satisfactory. Although it is well established that the police come to learn about most crimes through public reporting – normally by victims – rather than by their own efforts at detection, the victim was frequently ignored after the case had entered the criminal justice process. Research has suggested that victims who report incidents are often dissatisfied with the amount of information which they receive about the progress of 'their' case.[24] Until the last two decades, there was little support for victims in general or for victims of violence, where the formal legal process was particularly unhelpful (such as for rape victims or victims of 'domestic' violence). Once a crime was being dealt with officially, it appeared that all the interest centred on the offender (with his trial and sentence) and the victim became insignificant. This oversight had a number of damaging consequences. Victims who suffered psychological harm as a result of the crime were not only unaided; they were often further 'victimized' by the criminal justice process itself.

If victims feel that the response of the police is unsatisfactory to their crime report, they may well not bother to report incidents in the future. In this way, the public may become more cynical in its attitude to crime and law enforcement and may withdraw its support as reporters of crime and as potential witnesses. Certain serious crimes, such as rape and other assaults on women, may go unreported because of victims' fears that the case will not be handled sympathetically at various stages of the system. Few viewers of the television documentary on the Thames Valley Police in the early 1980s will forget the insensitive and hectoring manner of the officers who were filmed interviewing a young woman who reported that she had been raped. Despite considerable improvements since then in most police areas for dealing with rape reports and incidents of domestic violence, the damage done by insensitive handling of such cases is incalculable.

The problem is not restricted to the treatment of victims by the police. An infamous case in 1982, at Ipswich Crown Court, dealt with a man who gave a lift to a young woman hitch-hiker at night and raped her. The judge imposed a fine of £2,000 rather than a prison sentence, and justified this sentence by stating: 'I am not saying that a girl hitching home late at night should not be protected by the law, but she was guilty of a great deal of contributory negligence.'[25] The plight of women alleging rape, at court, is also a matter for concern. The cross-examination of them as to their previous sexual experience (which was supposedly restricted under section 2 of the Sexual Offences (Amendment) Act 1976) occurs all too frequently and can give the impression that it is the complainant who is on trial. For any victim, having to re-live the experience as a witness at the accused's trial can be painful and involve embarrassment, anxiety and sometimes humiliation. If the case results in an acquittal or an inadequate sentence (in the victim's eyes), this can lead to a feeling that it was not worth having bothered to report the offence in the first place. It is well established that the reporting rate for some crimes of violence (particularly for rape) is low. This is not simply because of suspicion of the criminal justice process itself, but it is clearly *a* factor which may inhibit the reporting of a serious offence, and this is to the detriment of everyone.[26]

Some of the early improvements in this area were not part of any centrally co-ordinated scheme to improve the lot of victims. Developments occurred more as a result of individual initiative (with some local authority support) aimed at remedying the obvious failure of the system to help victims. The pioneering work of Erin Pizzey in establishing refuges for victims of 'domestic' violence has been noted earlier.[27] Similarly, rape crisis centres were set up in the 1970s, initially in London and Birmingham, and more recently in close to fifty other areas.[28] The philosophy behind these centres was summed up by a volunteer worker at one of the longest-running centres which provides 24-hour support and counselling services to victims. She states:

The work of Rape Crisis Centres is based upon a diverse input of various feminist philosophies and individual women's experiences. However, the blanket term of radical feminism describes the feminism of many RCCs and their workers. Its main element is that it takes us to the experiences of other women. It demands that we realise and acknowledge how women feel, what difficulties they face and the struggles they are engaged in. We do not try to force our services upon them. When they wish it, we offer women the time and space to talk about their experiences in a setting where they are believed and supported.[29]

This response to female victims of violence is in sharp contrast to the treatment of rape victims in the criminal justice process. The bulk of rape crisis counselling is provided by telephone, and it relates to incidents of rape, other sexual assaults and child sexual abuse. The work of these centres also confirms the very low rate of reporting of rapes to the police.[30] The calls taken by RCCs also suggest that the victim frequently knows her assailant and is often attacked in her own home[31] The centres also have victims referred to them from the social services and from agencies within the criminal justice system. In addition to emotional support, centres may provide victims (which is not their preferred terminology) or 'survivors' with medical and legal advice. RCCs operate outside the criminal justice system and are dependent upon unpaid voluntary effort as well as employing paid workers. Their relations with the police are coloured by a good deal of suspicion, if not mistrust, of the police's handling of rape complaints and the lack of confidentiality which often accompanies the official processing of complaints. At worst, the police represent to RCCs and their clients a sexist, racist, male-dominated, authoritarian organization.[32]

In addition to the counselling provided by rape crisis centres, support for rape victims is also available through victim support schemes (VSS) which, because of their better relations with the police, tend to receive more referrals from them. For example, in 1985 the Metropolitan Police issued guidance to officers to refer rape victims, with the victim's permission, to a local VSS. This was part of a general reform within this police area of procedures for investigating rapes and dealing with victims.[33] Despite initial doubts about their suitability for dealing with rape victims, VSSs have extended their services so as to include referrals of this nature (and of other victims of violence) in addition to helping victims of property offences. In 1986, a separate VSS Working Party was set up to review training requirements for volunteers working with rape victims and other aspects of helping victims and liaising with other agencies.[34] Some women who are put off by the staunchly feminist image of Rape Crisis Centres may be more willing to receive counselling, support and assistance at court from VSS volunteers.

Victim Support has developed into a national organization since the first VSS was set up, in 1974, in Bristol. In 1977, national guidelines were issued for the founding of schemes and a national organization (formerly known as the National Association of Victim Support Schemes) was established in 1979.[35] As in most other countries where such schemes operate, VSSs in Britain depend largely on volunteers. Although there are state-run agencies to deal with the investigation of crime, the prosecution of suspects and the punishment of offenders, there is no official state agency for helping victims. Of course, the victim support movement depends on the co-operation of the established criminal justice agencies, and this is perhaps one of the reasons why the organization has adopted a less strident approach to other agencies (such as the police) than Rape Crisis Centres. Those who developed the early support schemes realized that the police would be willing to share information with volunteers only if they were assured that this incipient movement was dependable and not unduly critical.[36] Other reasons for a generally conciliatory attitude to official agencies include the need to attract government and other funding, and also to encourage volunteers from as wide a cross-section of society as possible. This cautious non-polemical approach has helped to build up confidence in the movement and to encourage referrals from other agencies, notably the police. This is particularly important in view of the approach taken by the victim support movement in not relying on the self-referral of victims, which would have been far too haphazard. Instead, the schemes have developed an 'outreach' service which involves actively contacting victims by calling on them, or by letter, or sometimes by telephone.[37] The emphasis is on short-term intensive support (where required), rather than providing long-term aid which might be more appropriately given by professional bodies.

As noted earlier, there is a central co-ordinating body (Victim Support) which enjoys close links with the Home Office and receives government funding. Each local scheme, run by a management committee, has a co-ordinator and volunteer workers who make contact with victims. The national Code of Practice ensures a degree of consistency in a support network which otherwise permits a fair amount of diversity. The code deals with issues such as training and the provision of services. Local schemes rely heavily on volunteers, and obviously some areas find it easier to recruit helpers than others. Ironically, some of the inner city areas with the highest rates of victimization may also be the same areas where recruitment is difficult from amongst the local population. Victim support schemes (there are now around 350) receive the vast majority of their referrals from the police, with whom the local co-ordinator liaises so as to obtain the relevant information. Decisions then have to be made about whom to contact and what form this should take. The support offered may include support aimed at helping the victim to deal with the emotional impact of the incident; it may involve giving practical advice to victims on the availability of services or compensation; or it may take the form of assistance with crime prevention measures or repairs which have been necessitated by the incident. Although early schemes tended to concentrate on victims of property offences (notably burglary), we have seen how they came to be involved increasingly with helping victims of violence also.

As the victim support movement depends heavily on the police for its referrals, it deals almost exclusively with reported and recorded offences. (Rape Crisis Centres are not limited in this way, but they deal with a much narrower range of offences.) It could be argued that most serious crimes will come to the attention of the police and, in turn, to VSSs and that the dependency on the police does not lead to any serious bias in the cases dealt with by the scheme. This is broadly true, but some offences which appear fairly trivial or go unreported for other reasons (such as dislike of the police) may also involve victims who might benefit from support and advice. Offences which are particularly common and distressing in some urban areas, such as vandalism and racial abuse, may go unreported (or unrecorded) and escape the attentions of victim support. Formerly, schemes were criticized for concentrating too extensively on particular types of victim (such as the elderly or women) who were seen to represent the popular 'image' of victims of crime, rather than spreading their efforts more widely across the whole spectrum of those who may benefit from victim support services. This practice probably contributed to the solid, conventional reputation of the movement and helped to inspire confidence both at government level and amongst local police forces. Victim support was not tainted by association with 'undeserving' victims or involved in areas which were inimical to law and order policies. Of course, not all victims fit this popular image and the extension of support services to a wider category of victims is a welcome development.

This quietly cautious approach by the victim support movement has been successful, at a political level, by being ostentatiously non-political. Accordingly, it is a movement which appeals to all. The movement has developed and flourished during a period of unbroken Conservative rule at Westminster, in which much emphasis has been placed on 'law and order' and getting tough with criminals. A concern for victims provides the 'softer face' of official policy at a financial cost which is relatively modest in comparison to the expenditure on the police and the penal system. Also, being rooted in voluntary efforts, the victim support movement has appealed to the ideology of successive governments.

Victim Support has also played its part in developing a rapport with the government and criminal justice agencies. Unlike the United States' victim movement, it has eschewed an outspoken approach to victims' rights and the punishment of offenders. For example, it does not campaign for tougher penalties for offenders and so avoids a right-wing or reactionary image. Similarly, by building up a harmonious working relationship with the police, the movement is not seen as anti-establishment or too radical. In view of both the inability to reduce crime, and the undoubted need to offer emotional and practical support to many of its victims, most people agree that victim support schemes provide invaluable services. By attracting government funding, the movement has secured the implicit acceptance by the government that helping victims is a legitimate concern of the state.

Victim Support does not have the resources to provide a comprehensive service to assist victims and witnesses appearing in court, but there have been some developments in this area. It is widely acknowledged that many victims become more disenchanted with the criminal justice system as 'their' case progresses through the system to trial.[38] Lack of information (both before and at the trial), delays, the alien nature of court proceedings and the poor provision of services and facilities at court are just some of the issues which upset victims.[39] Victim Support has recently extended its services in a small number of pilot areas so as to provide help to victims attending Crown Courts, and there are proposals to extend this incipient witness support scheme more widely.[40] Once again, a low-key approach is essential if this scheme is to be accepted by the main criminal justice agencies. There have been criticisms that witness support at court could be inimical to impartiality and somehow suggest official support for the prosecution witnesses. Naturally, any suggestion that the case is being prejudged must be avoided, and volunteers must be careful not to convey any such impression.

This new programme of witness support received a favourable comment from the Royal Commission on Criminal Justice in its recent report.[41] The report emphasized the importance of victims and other witnesses being prepared to testify in court and of giving them the necessary support to minimize the unpleasantness of this experience. In reference to the experimental witness support schemes, it was stated that priority should be given to the setting up of such schemes in all Crown Court centres. The report stated (at para. 39):

An important feature of the witness support schemes . . . is that they help to prevent a witness from feeling isolated in what may well be unfamiliar and intimidating surroundings. This may be particularly necessary when the victim goes into the witness box . . . We judge that it is perfectly acceptable in such circumstances for the witness to be accompanied by a friend or supporter who sits in the body of the court, although he or she should not accompany the witness into the witness box nor sit close to the witness box while the witness is giving evidence. This is to avoid any suggestion that the witness is not giving his or her evidence unaided. We understand that it may still be the case in some Crown Court centres that a friend or supporter of the witness will be excluded from the court or placed in the public gallery. This seems to us to be wrong: the admission of the witness's friend or supporter to the body of the court though not to the witness box itself seems to us to be an acceptable compromise.

Although the police depend on victims to bring offences to their attention and the state relies on victims to give evidence, there has been a feeling that relatively little is done by the state to compensate victims for what has happened to them. We have seen how the state has provided some financial assistance to the victim support movement, but it has also kept sufficient distance from the scheme so as to refute any suggestion that the state has a duty to help victims. A similarly tentative approach has been evident in relation to state-funded compensation. The compensation of victims had been seen, generally, as a function of the civil process rather than a concern of the state. But, in reality, this process offered few victims much hope of success, on account of the costs involved and the lack of funds of the majority of offenders. The government in the early 1960s came under pressure (notably from the 'Justice' organization) to review its role in relation to victims of crime, especially victims of violence, and this led to the publication of a White Paper in 1964 on this subject.[42] In 1964, the Criminal Injuries Compensation Scheme was established on a non-statutory footing, but the White Paper had made it clear that, by paying compensation on an *ex gratia* basis, the government was not accepting any duty to make such payments to those who were victimized by another person's acts. The scheme was restricted to victims of violent crime and it was stressed that payments would be made only to 'innocent' victims.

A distinct advantage of a state scheme, as administered by the Criminal Injuries Compensation Board since 1964, is that it does not depend on a victim being able to identify a particular offender – it should be remembered that many offenders are never caught. Despite its rather narrow scope, it does represent some acknowledgement of the state's role in helping victims in addition to simply relying on them to make initial complaints about offences and to testify to their commission.[43] More recently, the state's obligations towards victims in this respect has been recognized at international level by the European Convention on the Compensation of Victims of Violent Crimes.[44] The

Criminal Injuries Compensation Scheme was placed on a statutory basis under sections 109–17 of the Criminal Justice Act 1988, which also set out the terms and conditions on which awards are to be made by the Criminal Injuries Compensation Board (CICB). The CICB was replaced by a new Criminal Injuries Compensation Authority in 1994.

The Criminal Injuries Compensation Scheme has been criticized for being too narrowly focused on offences against the person. Whilst this policy has helped to make the scheme relatively inexpensive, it has led to accusations of tokenism, as the vast majority of offences committed each year do not involve personal injury or death. There is also the more basic philosophical question of why this particular group of victims should be eligible for compensation by the state whilst others are not. Is this an arbitrary, pragmatic distinction or is it based on some characteristics of this group of victims which makes them more deserving of compensation? It could well be argued that the suffering caused by personal injury cases is more acute than other forms of victimization and that, in view of limited state resources, this group should be given priority. This argument does not, however, deal with the issue of why criminal injuries should be treated as a separate case from other forms of personal injury, such as those caused by accident or disease.[45]

Other criticisms of the scheme refer to the arbitrary distinction between 'innocent' and other victims of criminal injuries.[46] The White Paper of 1964[47] made specific reference to the public's feelings of responsibility towards and sympathy with *innocent* victims. From the outset, the victim's own criminal record or way of life could disqualify him or her from receiving a compensation award, as could a failure to report the offence to the police. It has to be accepted that certain victims may be more deserving than others; for example, a victim who provoked the offender's assault by verbal abuse or taunts may attract our sympathy less than an apparently blameless victim. But, this distinction can be very subjective and contentious. By way of criticism of the innocent/undeserving victim dichotomy, it can be objected that the harm done to the victim, for which a compensation award is being claimed, may be equally severe in the case of someone who is adjudged not to be entirely blameless. There are sound policy reasons for wishing to encourage victims to report serious offences to the police promptly. But there are certain types of violence, such as sexual and domestic assaults, which victims may either find difficulty in reporting (at least initially), or be fearful that the reporting of the offence might lead to further psychological damage. Although incidents of domestic violence are no longer absolutely barred from coming within the ambit of the scheme, there are still practical restrictions on such claims and they are successful only in very serious instances.

A further problem for many victims is lack of knowledge about the scheme and about how to make a claim. Reliance on the police can lead to unfairness as the police may have their own 'rough and ready' criteria for deciding which victims are deserving. Some improvement in the dissemination of information to victims about the scheme has come about through the development of the victim support movement. Predictably, claims have increased sharply in number in recent times although a smaller proportion of claimants are now successful.[48] Of the £909 million paid out since the scheme began in 1964, £405 million has been paid out in the 1990–3 period. The CICB's annual report for 1992–3 revealed a 6 per cent increase from the previous year's record payout, with an annual payout of around £152 million.

In 1992, the Home Secretary indicated that the government intended to introduce a non-statutory, flat-rate (tariff) scheme which was designed to reduce significantly the rapidly rising cost of compensating victims. This new scheme was attacked from the outset by critics who claimed that it was both unfair and unconstitutional. An application was made by eleven trade unions and other bodies for judicial review of the Home Secretary's decision to implement the tariff scheme. As a result, the House of Lords held that the Home Secretary acted unlawfully in introducing this new scheme while the existing statutory scheme had not been repealed.[49] A new scheme is finally to be introduced in 1996, under which a fixed sum is allocated to each type of injury. In addition there will be a sum to compensate for loss of earnings after 28 weeks, and there will also be something for loss of future earnings, pension rights and for 'special expenses'.

Just as criminology tended to concentrate on the ætiology of offending rather than on the impact of crime upon victims, penology has been preoccupied (as the name implies) with the punishment of offenders. Occasionally, as in the middle of the twentieth century, the notion of treatment has gained ground, but the central concept in the state's response to crime has been that of punishment. More recently, greater attention has been paid to reparation and compensation, so as to reflect the growing awareness that too often in the past the position of victims has been virtually ignored. We have looked at a number of reasons for this recent growth of interest in victims and it is now relevant to consider developments in the sentencing system which have improved their position.

The state's response to law-breaking is expressed by the collection of measures available to the criminal courts which we refer to collectively as the sentencing system. The application of these sentences, which are decided upon by judges or magistrates subject to statutory and common law constraints, can be conveniently called the 'penal' system.[50]

However, not all measures available to the courts are 'penal' in nature; for example, sentences for the mentally disordered offender may be more concerned with treatment rather than punishment. But generally the concept of punishment has dominated thinking about the response to offending. This subject has received considerable attention from moral philosophers who have analysed the ethical basis for the state's use of coercive measures against those who break the law.[51]

The two main groups of views as to what justifies the state's infliction of punishment on offenders are retributivism and utilitarianism. Retributivism is concerned with the moral justification of punishment, in terms of the requirements of a just social order, whilst utilitarians support punishment by reference to its perceived beneficial consequences (for example, in reducing crime, or protecting the public). It is arguably futile to attempt to separate retributive and utilitarian ideas in a rigid way: the broad ethical basis for state action is a mixture of retributive and utilitarian thinking. But the principle of 'retribution in distribution'[52] helps to prevent the morally unacceptable use of penal measures either against those who lack culpability, or in a way which is disproportionate to the nature and impact of the offending conduct. It should be appreciated that punishment involves a number of issues: such as, what justifies the state's use of coercive measures against an offender? Which groups should be punished and which should not be? How severely (and by what methods) should punishment be exacted?[53] Rather than supporting retributivism as opposed to utilitarianism (or vice versa), it can be argued that the two theories provide us with solutions to different problems. Instead of a strict adherence to either of these two main groups of views, some sort of synthesis of elements of both is a defensible approach to the issue of punishment.

The sentencing system in England and Wales has tended to comprise a number of different penal values. There have always been elements of retribution in our penal process, but the notion of deterrence (both general and individual) has also been deeply ingrained in the judicial consciousness. The rehabilitative aims of sentencing have also enjoyed some popularity from time to time, but have tended to suffer from the 'nothing works' cynicism which surfaces when the success of penal measures is evaluated solely in terms of reconviction rates. The sentencer has been able to exercise a wide discretion under the English sentencing system in deciding upon the sentence for any particular offender. As long as he acted within his statutory powers and paid some heed to the very general common law principles (where relevant), a sentencer was entitled to decide each case on an individual basis. Supporters of this wide judicial discretion argued that it enabled sentencers to apply whichever penal or utilitarian value was appropriate in the individual case in question. There can be little doubt that there is *some* attractiveness in the idea that offenders committing similar offences may receive different sentences, so as to reflect different purposes of punishment. For example, one burglar might be thought likely to respond to a rehabilitative measure, whilst another might be perceived as in need of a deterrent sentence. But this 'free choice' approach has also been heavily criticized for its arbitrariness and for the disparities which it produced in practice.[54] The concept of judicial discretion in sentencing often seemed to justify judges following their own individual penal philosophies, which in turn was inimical to the development of consistent and principled sentencing policies.

The same critics argued that sentencers needed a coherent basis for choosing between the competing values (such as rehabilitation, deterrence or retribution) which underlie the available sentencing options.[55] The views of these critics were reflected, at least in part, in the Criminal Justice Act 1991 which sought to restrict judicial discretion and promote 'proportionality' as the guiding principle in sentencing. As a result of this legislation, sentences are to reflect (in most cases) the seriousness of the crime, with offenders receiving their just deserts. Much of the impetus for this attempt at restricting discretion came from a growing exasperation with disproportionate sentences, which were often given in the name of deterrence, and the continuing use of quite lengthy custodial sentences for non-violent offenders. The relatively severe treatment by the courts of the persistent property offender was widely believed to be a major factor responsible for England and Wales having one of the highest prison populations in Europe.[56] The continuing problem of prison overcrowding (and serious rioting), the relative failure of non-custodial alternatives in tackling these problems, and an international trend towards stricter control of sentencing discretion all contributed to the government's decision to intervene more directly in sentencing policy. Its intentions were articulated in the White Paper, *Crime, Justice and Protecting the Public*,[57] which proposed a radical reform of sentencing practice by establishing a clearly defined set of principles. It was stated:

> The aim of the Government's proposals is better justice through a more consistent approach to sentencing, so that convicted criminals get their 'just deserts'. The severity of the sentence of the court should be directly related to the seriousness of the offence. Most offenders can be punished by financial penalties – by paying compensation to their victims and by fines. When offences are too serious to be properly punished by financial penalties alone, the courts have a choice of community penalties, such as probation or community service, or of custody . . . The legislation will give guidance in general terms on when these punishments should be used.[58]

The White Paper explained that these reforms were designed to create a coherent framework for sentencing decisions and to promote greater consistency 'so that victims are compensated, the public protected and offenders receive their just deserts'.[59] The government specifically rejected the deterrent principle as a basis for judicial sentencing, despite the 'immediate appeal' of the concept in abstract terms. It argued that as most offenders act on impulse, and not by any rational calculation of the risks of being apprehended and punished, it is futile to pass sentence on this basis.[60] The recognition of this fact signified an important break with traditional sentencing practice. These proposals for a new legislative framework based on proportionality were enacted (to a large extent) by the Criminal Justice Act 1991.[61] Due to adverse criticism by judges and academics of some of its more troublesome sections, this major piece of legislation has already been amended and, some would argue, seriously weakened by the Criminal Justice Act 1993.[62]

This is not the place for an evaluation of the proportionality approach and its reliance on neo-retributive principles.[63] Some tenets of recent penal philosophy, as espoused by the White Paper, deserve widespread support, such as the rejection of deterrence as a basis for sentencing decisions. The use of lengthy custodial sentences for serious offences of violence, but not for property and less serious crimes, is also unexceptionable. But it might be questioned whether the emphasis on 'just deserts' is entirely defensible. There are other quite legitimate values, such as rehabilitation, which need to be acknowledged and it may be asked why sentencers should not be able to choose which aim is uppermost in any particular case. Moreover, the proportionality approach presupposes that there is a simple dichotomy between those who break the law and those who do not. In reality, law-breaking is much more common than official figures suggest and many corporate and 'white-collar' offences escape a penal response. Those who are processed by the criminal justice system as a result of their offending tend to be young, male and most frequently from the more dis-advantaged sections of society. This suggests, perhaps, that those who offend do so not from choice in each case, but also as a result of inequalities created by social and political policies. How realistic is it for the sentencing system to proceed against each offender on the basis of 'just deserts' and to take little account of individual factors relating to the offender?[64]

The objective of compensating victims through the sentencing system also received support from the White Paper, *Crime, Justice and Protecting the Public*,[65] where it was stated that 'there was considerable support for compensation orders and the priority which the courts are now required to give them in considering the possibility of making compensation orders in all suitable cases.' Since 1972, criminal courts have been able to make compensation orders when exercising their sentencing powers. The Criminal Justice Act 1972 gave courts the power to order an offender to pay compensation for any personal loss or damage resulting from the offence.[66] It was stated in *Inwood*[67] that the aim of such an order is to give the victim a straightforward and effective method of obtaining compensation from an offender who can afford to pay, without having to resort to expensive civil litigation. Initially, this power was available to the courts only *in addition* to any other sentence which it imposed on the offender but, since 1982, a court can make a compensation order 'instead of or in addition to' dealing with him in any other way.[68] So as to encourage the use of this power by the courts, section 104 of the Criminal Justice Act 1988 provides that a court shall give reasons, when passing sentence, if it chooses not to make a compensation order when it has the power to do so. It is worth noting that although an order can be made without any formal application being made by the victim to the court, it is not advisable for victims to rely on the courts to consider this issue as a matter of course.[69]

The use of compensation orders, and the impact of the Criminal Justice Act 1988, was the subject of recent research by the Home Office Research and Planning Unit.[70] The researchers found that the new provision led to a sizeable increase in the use of orders in cases of assault in both the magistrates' courts and the Crown Courts. As the courts had also been given closer guidance on the amount to award for specific injuries (based on the Criminal Injuries Compensation Board figures), the researchers also assessed the degree of adherence by the courts to this guidance. It was found that in the case of serious injuries sustained by victims, the courts frequently awarded compensation which was well below the recommended guidelines. In relation to minor injuries, there was closer adherence to the suggested levels. The researchers also found that, in the case of property offences, the 1988 legislation had made much less impact on sentencers, and the increase in the use of compensation orders was only slight.

Although an order may be made by a court even without an application by the victim, it appears that the absence of a specific claim is the most common reason for sentencers deciding not to make an award. The Home Office research stated that 'this underlines the need for the police and the Crown Prosecution Service to ensure that relevant details are provided to the court.'[71] In other words, it should not be the responsibility of the victim alone to provide this information to the court; it should become part of the formal mechanism of the criminal justice process.[72]

Sentencers have always been reticent about making a compensation order on its own (that is, not in addition to another sentence), and this reluctance was also evident from the Home Office research. The attitude of sentencers is not really surprising, as the present law tends to obfuscate the (arguably) distinct notions of punishment and compensation. If a compensation order is made by a court as the sole method of dealing with an offender, it gives the impression of being his punishment for the offence. It is understandable if sentencers find difficulty in accepting the compensation order as a measure in its own right, rather than as something which can be added to the penalty which they otherwise wish to impose. If compensation alone is awarded, it might be argued that the criminal court is merely fulfilling the role of a civil court, albeit in a more expeditious and convenient way for the victim. Traditionally, the concern of criminal courts has been with punishing offenders, and the use of compensation orders can be more easily reconciled with the conventional approach of sentencers where they are additional to other sentences, and not used instead of them.

Of course, this raises fundamental questions about the nature of punishment. It must be borne in mind that very few victims have the inclination or resources to sue the person who inflicted harm on them, and therefore a compensation order leads to an imposition which the offender may otherwise have escaped. To this extent, it can be argued that the sentencer is not only compensating the victim, but also penalizing the offender.[73] But this rationalization is not entirely convincing. The use of the criminal process against, and the imposition of a sentence on, the offender also signifies the public condemnation of the offending conduct, as well as protecting the victim's interests. If compensation is awarded on its own, the victim's expectations may (or may not) be satisfied, but it is hard to see how the public can be satisfied with such an outcome.[74]

Before the revival of interest in the position of the victim, the interests of the state were totally predominant in the sentencing of offenders. It would be ironic if the modern emphasis on compensation for the victim were to lead, in turn, to the public-interest element in the prosecution and punishment of offenders being virtually ignored in selected cases of a less serious nature. But it seems that the reluctance of sentencers to use the compensation order as a measure in its own right will ensure that the offender's conduct will continue to be viewed as a wrong against the public as a whole and not just the victim. Whilst some have argued that compensation by the offender should be the main purpose of the state's response to criminal conduct[75] and that traditional penal responses are largely ineffective, few would accept such a point of view. Compensation or reparation by the offender is clearly an important goal of the modern 'penal' system, but it is not the only, or even the most important, one.

There are other utilitarian aims of punishment which are worth pursuing for the good of society as a whole and not just the victim. Furthermore, a penal response based primarily on compensation rather than culpability (or just deserts) would punish offenders for the chance outcome of their conduct rather than for their evil intentions, and this would not be a defensible or logical guiding principle.

Sentencers most likely recognize that in exercising their powers they are protecting the interests of all of the public and not just the victim. This may account perhaps for their continuing reluctance to give priority to a compensation order where they wish to impose such an order together with a fine. Section 35(4A) of the Powers of Criminal Courts Act 1973 states that where a court considers that it is appropriate to combine these financial measures, yet it also thinks that the offender lacks the means to pay both, priority should be given to compensation. The Home Office research referred to earlier suggests that courts frequently disregard this statutory provision and fail to give precedence to compensation where a fine is also imposed.

A compensation order may be made by a court in respect of personal injury, loss or damage, and this includes where a crime causes the victim distress and anxiety.[76] Section 104(1) of the Criminal Justice Act 1988 introduced a further amendment to the 1973 legislation so as to enable compensation for 'funeral expenses or bereavement in respect of death resulting from any such offence, other than a death due to an accident arising out of the presence of a motor vehicle on a road'. A Crown Court is not restricted in the amount which it may award, but magistrates cannot make compensation orders in excess of £5,000 for any offence. In deciding on whether to make an order, and on the amount of an order, sentencers must take account of the offender's means.[77] It is bad sentencing practice to make an order if there is real doubt as to whether the offender can afford to pay compensation.[78] It has also been held by the Court of Appeal that compensation orders are not to be used so as to enable offenders 'to buy themselves out of the penalties for crime'.[79] For example, if it is thought that the crime merits a custodial sentence, the offender should not escape this punishment simply because he has the ability to pay compensation.[80] This principle illustrates once again that the state's response to offending, as reflected in the sentencing system, encapsulates other important values in addition to reparative aims.

This chapter has focused largely on the growing interest in victims in Britain since the 1970s, whilst briefly noting the parallel developments in other countries. It is worth emphasizing that there has been a similar upsurge of interest in victims in Europe and in North America, and that this has been reflected in a number of official statements and legal instruments during the 1980s and 1990s. For example, in 1985, a charter of victims' rights was adopted by the United Nations General Assembly, known as the UN Declaration on the Basic Principles of Justice for Victims of Crime and Abuse of Power (see below). The Council of Europe has also sought to ameliorate the position of victims, notably by means of the European Convention on the Compensation of Victims of Violent Crime (1983), the Recommendation on the Position of the Victim in the Framework of Criminal Law and Procedure (1985)[81] and the Recommendation on Assistance to Victims and Prevention of Victimization (1987).[82]

In contrast to the more political 'rights-based' approach of North American reforms, the European response has been to press for practical improvements in victim services both within the criminal justice system and outside it.[83] The European Convention on the Compensation of Victims of Violent Crimes relates to the provision of compensation, directly out of state funds, for victims of violent crime. Whilst a very important statement, it did not cover compensation for non-violent crime, and it did not help those who needed assistance immediately after an offence. The Council of Europe's recommendation on improving the victim's position in the framework of criminal law and procedure was wider in scope than the 1983 Convention, but was concerned only with the response of the criminal justice system to victims. In short, neither of these statements dealt with the wider aspects of victims' needs and the types of assistance they require.

For this reason, a separate Council of Europe document in 1987 dealt with assistance to victims and the prevention of victimization, concentrating on services for victims outside the framework of criminal procedure and apart from state compensation.[84] It recommended that governments of member states conduct research to find out the rate of victimization and the extent of victims' needs, increase the public's awareness of these matters, and inform the public of the services which are available to help victims. As part of this public information, governments were called upon to improve access by victims to these services and encourage the police to assist in referring victims, where appropriate, to support schemes. It was urged that victims (and their families) receive: prompt help to meet their immediate needs; advice to prevent repeat victimization; continuing medical treatment, counselling or other material support; and information about their rights (including the right to compensation) and about assistance during the criminal justice process. Governments were also asked to set up (or develop) services for victims both generally and for special groups, such as children, and for victims of particular offences such as domestic violence, rape and racially motivated assaults. Where such services were provided by voluntary organizations, governments were called upon to encourage these efforts and support them with professional help and training. It was also the responsibility of governments to implement crime prevention measures and improve public awareness of these issues.

The Seventh United Nations Congress on the Prevention of Crime and the Treatment of Offenders[85] recognized the need, at both international and national levels, for more effective support for victims of crime. It recommended that the United Nations General Assembly should adopt the Declaration of Basic Principles of Justice for Victims of Crime and Abuse of Power and this recommendation was duly accepted.[86] In addition to emphasizing the entitlement of victims to fair treatment and to compensation, this charter also stated that the responsiveness of legal and other services for victims should be improved by:

(a) Informing victims of their role and the scope, timing and progress of the proceedings and of the disposition of their cases, especially where serious crimes are involved and where they have requested such information;
(b) Allowing the views and concerns of victims to be presented and considered at appropriate stages of the proceedings where their personal interests are affected, without prejudice to the accused and consistent with the relevant national criminal justice system;
(c) Providing proper assistance to victims throughout the legal process;
(d) Taking measures to minimise inconvenience to victims, protect their privacy, when necessary, and ensure their safety as well as that of their families and witnesses on their behalf, from intimidation and retaliation;
(e) Avoiding unnecessary delay in the disposition of cases and the execution of orders or decrees granting awards to victims.[87]

In Britain, the Victim's Charter (1990) is the government's expression of its commitment to improving the position of victims, and it also states what victims are entitled to expect from the relevant support agencies and the criminal justice system.[88] Despite the reference in the subtitle of this charter to the 'rights' of victims, the document does not create legally enforceable rights. It is mainly concerned with improving services and information for victims at each stage of the criminal justice process. Accordingly, it is stated that the police should provide a prompt and courteous response to reports of crimes. They should also make available to all victims the Home Office leaflet *Victims of Crime* which informs them of how the court can make compensation orders against offenders and of how awards may be made under the Criminal Injuries Compensation Scheme.[89] Similarly, the charter provides details on the working of victim support schemes, criminal proceedings, going to court as a witness and giving evidence, and protection for victims from convicted offenders.[90]

These general statements of concern and support for victims, both in Europe and in Britain, are to be welcomed. Of course, they can also be criticized for failing to develop enforceable rights for victims and for leaving too much to the discretion of professional groups within the criminal justice system and to the efforts of voluntary workers. There is also a concern that if the interests of victims are to be more forcefully asserted, that this does not led to any diminution of the rights of defendants. A further criticism is that general statements, such as the Victim's Charter, do not go far enough in assisting the victims of crime. It can be argued that the government's support for victims appears less convincing when viewed in the context of its attempts to replace the former Criminal Injuries Compensation Scheme with a cheaper, tariff-based system.

In other areas also, it seems that the plight of victims has not improved significantly. For example, the reforms laid down by the Criminal Justice Act 1991, which were designed to expedite child abuse cases and reduce court room stress for such victims, do not appear to be working effectively.[91] A recent survey[92] by a charitable organization estimated that upwards of three-quarters of a million children in Britain may suffer long-term psychological damage through their exposure to domestic violence. It is clearly not enough for the government to offer such victims vague statements of support, as set out in the Victim's Charter. What is needed is practical and financial support, such as better access to alternative housing, increased funding for women's refuges, improvements to social and welfare benefits, and a more informed response from professional agencies. It is in these areas that the performance of the government, and its commitment to helping victims, should be judged.

3

Crime Surveys: Shedding Light on the 'Dark Figure'

It is widely accepted that official crime statistics, based on offences reported to and recorded by the police, are a poor reflection of all the crimes that are actually committed each year. One possible response to this deficiency might be to argue that as most serious offences get reported and recorded, it is not worth bothering with the relatively trivial ones which escape official attention. But, to accept such a view, we should first have to establish that it is only minor offences that go unreported and unrecorded. There is evidence that this is not the case. Also, a more reliable method of measuring the crime rate is required if we are more fully to understand (and act upon) the changing patterns of crime and victimization. For example, a dramatic increase in official crime might be based on a change in reporting trends by victims and other members of the public. Another weakness of official figures is that they tell us nothing about the victim and the effects of crime amongst different groups in society. If crime statistics are meant to be a barometer of the 'moral health' of a society, then it makes sense to use a more sophisticated instrument for measuring this well-being than that supplied by police statistics.

The 'dark figure' of unreported or unrecorded crime can be investigated by research techniques such as self-report and victim studies. Asking sample groups (especially of young people), in conditions of anonymity, about crimes they have committed, is a useful research technique, although not without its concomitant methodological problems. A more useful method is the crime or victimization survey. This is based on a sample of the population (either regional or national) being interviewed by a trained researcher using a general 'screening' questionnaire, about whether they have been victims of crime within a specific period, usually approximately twelve months. If the respondents have been victims of crime (or repeat victims), details of the incident(s) are recorded as part of a second questionnaire on a 'victim form'. Further 'follow-up' information can also be gained from victims about the effects of the offence(s) upon them. In addition to surveying crimes committed, and whether these were reported by victims to the police, victim studies can also provide valuable information about the characteristics of victims in relation to age, gender, social status and the housing in which they live. They can also tell us about the lifestyle of victims, fear of crime in general, attitudes to the punishment of offenders, opinions about the police, reasons for non-reporting of crime, and the types of crime prevention measures employed (or not employed) by respondents. In order to contrast the crime figures derived from this type of survey with official rates of offending, the results of the survey can be 'multiplied up' from the sample to give an overall crime rate that represents the total population (either regional or national).

Obviously victimization surveys are not free from methodological drawbacks, although they are being refined constantly as this research technique has become more widely practised and accepted. One problem is in relation to achieving a sample which adequately represents the total population and does not exclude specific groups in society. The sample has to be of sufficient size to enable reliable estimates to be made about the crime rate for the whole population, and there is bound to be sampling error. If a particular type of crime is uncommon, the estimates derived from a survey will not be very reliable. The results of the interviews are dependent on human memory, which is fallible, and on the candour of the respondent. A twelve-month period is quite a long one in which to recall all incidents of a criminal nature. Incidents may well be recorded in the survey which did not, in fact, fall within the relevant period, whilst some which did fall within the period may have been forgotten. Incidents may not be disclosed by respondents either due to embarrassment (for example, in relation to sexual and other assaults) or fear of another member of their household being made aware of a previously undisclosed incident.

So the need for crime or victimization surveys as a corrective to official crime statistics occurred when recorded crime rates began to increase significantly over the last thirty years or more. Although the first national crime survey in Britain took place in 1982 (see below), the General Household Survey had included a question about burglary throughout the previous decade. The use of victim surveys, however, originated in the United States of America. For this reason, it is appropriate to start by considering the American experience.

The National Crime Survey in the United States was developed to investigate the annual rates of victimization of individuals and households for the offences of theft, car-related theft, burglary, robbery, assault and rape. Although originally supported by the Law Enforcement Assistance Administration, this research initiative was switched to the Bureau of Judicial Statistics in 1979.[1] The origins of the

National Crime Survey can be found in the work of the President's Commission on Law Enforcement and Administration of Justice (the 'Crime Commission') in the 1960s, which sought more reliable crime figures than those provided, for recorded crime, by the FBI's Uniform Crime Reporting System. An early survey by the National Opinion Research Centre, in 1966, suggested that there was indeed a large 'dark figure' of unreported and unrecorded crime that did not find its way into the official statistics. Although victimization research was relatively unsophisticated at this time, such studies persuaded politicians and researchers that there was much potential to be developed. This research initiative was taken up by the National Crime Survey Programme which, in 1972, was launched with a nation-wide survey of randomly selected households, after earlier studies had been conducted in selected major cities.[2]

Despite the many advantages of victimization surveys over official (recorded) statistics, it should be borne in mind that such surveys cannot provide an exact measure of crime. Inevitably, all crime figures will contain an element of distortion. As Stephen Fienberg states:

Any set of crime statistics, including those of the [National Crime] survey, involves some evaluative, institutional processing of people's reports. Concepts, definitions, quantitative models, and theories must be adjusted to the fact that the data are not some objectively observable universe of 'criminal acts', but rather those events defined, captured, and processed as such by some institutional mechanism.[3]

But the National Crime Survey (NCS) was able to shed light on the dark figure of unreported crime. Moreover, this research was able to provide information about the impact of crime on its victims, multiple victimization, and the characteristics of offenders and their relationships (where relevant) with victims. The value of this research was increased when surveys were repeated at regular intervals. The methodological problems encountered in the studies, and the solutions adopted by the researchers working on the NCS have been of inestimable value to social scientists in other countries, including Britain.[4] Researchers had to consider the extent of memory failure for respondents in surveys, and the best period of time to be covered by a survey for the purpose of recalling incidents. The phrasing of questions about criminal incidents was another area that needed refining so as to ensure that the respondent clearly understood the type of offences being asked about, and also that these incidents corresponded to the definitions of crimes in official statistics.

For example, it was found in early research (in 1970–1) that the recall rates for incidents of personal victimization were heavily dependent on the offender–victim relationship. If the offender was not known to the victim, the recall rate for such incidents was high. But where the offender was known (or even related) to the victim, the reporting rate was low. This has considerable implications for victimization surveys, as it is well established that assaults and other acts of violence commonly occur in circumstances where the victim knows or is related to the offender. For this reason, recall rates for assaults in crime surveys may well be a considerable undercount of the actual number of offences which occurred during the relevant period. On the other hand, the number of property offences recalled by respondents in surveys is likely to be a more accurate reflection of the number of incidents which actually occurred.

In choosing the recall period for a victimization survey there has to be some compromise between cost and accuracy, as shorter survey periods require larger samples. Early United States studies tested recall accuracy by comparing survey data with information from police records, with samples of known victims being taken from police incident records. Despite some problems with this approach, it enabled researchers to compare the description of an incident (if recalled) by a respondent in the survey to the interviewer with the official report which was made, at the time of the incident, to the police. It was found that a respondent was more likely to recall accurately *when* an incident occurred if the survey period was relatively short. The period of time covered by the survey was less critical if it simply wanted to ascertain *whether* an incident had occurred at all, rather than how long ago.[5]

Further methodological problems were considered in relation to the choice of the respondent in a household. Is it an individual or a household that is the target respondent for interviewers? If it is simply a matter of interviewing any adult in the chosen household who answers the door when the interviewer calls, this can lead to some bias in the results obtained for 'personal' offences. For example, the person at home is perhaps less likely to be in employment or education and this may affect their chances of personal (as opposed to household) victimization.

After assessing these methodological problems and studying the results obtained from the local surveys, the first National Crime Survey was conducted in the United States in 1972, taking a national sample of 72,000 households (for the NCS) and 15,000 businesses (for the Commercial Victimization Survey). A further sample was taken in each of twenty-six large cities. (The collection of data for the Commercial Victimization Survey was suspended in 1977.) The data generated by the NCS research made a significant contribution to the understanding of trends and patterns of crime and the distribution of victimization.

Although far from perfect in execution, this initiative was to encourage social scientists in other countries to adopt similar programmes of research. The value of continuing NCS research was not in simply producing estimates of crime and victimization to set against official statistics, but rather in providing 'a range of social indicators'.[6] In other words, victimization studies were able to assist the understanding of the effects of crime, both on victims and on society in general. Unlike official statistics on crime, surveys offered some insight into the distribution of risk of victimization and repeat victimization. In addition to this objective information, questions could be added to gauge the subjective opinions of respondents on a range of crime and law enforcement issues. For example, whatever the objective risk of being a victim of a 'mugging', it may be a pressing social problem if a large proportion of the population live in fear of this crime. It was claimed that a good reason for continuing NCS research lay in the fact that 'it could help to illuminate [American] society's concepts of crime and the moral order, and it could help to provide a factual foundation for a reassessment of that moral order'.[7]

It was probably inevitable that victimization surveys would be seen not merely as a method of describing or measuring crime and victimization, but would also have a part to play in the analysis of these phenomena. At the outset, the NCS programme was largely descriptive in its orientation. But as survey research has been developed and used in other countries it has come to include an increasingly explanatory or analytical dimension. In other words, victimization surveys are not simply interested in counting crimes and victims as a complement to official statistics, but in explaining patterns and trends in criminal behaviour and analysing the individual and social reaction to crime.

The British Crime Survey Programme

Although the British Crime Survey (BCS) in 1982 was the first detailed national British victimization survey, it should be noted that the General Household Survey also included questions about victimization throughout the 1970s.[8] There were also earlier local surveys and studies of victimization.[9] The national survey was planned in the early 1980s, primarily as a descriptive research tool, to provide a more accurate measure of crime and victimization rates than that supplied by police statistics. It was also hoped that it would be of assistance to crime prevention initiatives by highlighting the groups most at risk of victimization. In the words of Mayhew and Hough,[10] the national survey 'promised a more informed picture of crime which might help create a more balanced climate of opinion about law and order'. It is also fair to say that the impetus for this research coincided with (or was even fuelled by) an increasing concern with the whole subject of victims in the criminal justice process.

The first British Crime Survey was conducted in 1982 and there have been successive 'sweeps' of the survey in 1984, 1988, 1992, 1994 and 1996. The survey was designed and developed by the Home Office Research and Planning Unit in conjunction with an independent survey organization. (A number of market research companies have been involved in BCS fieldwork and data preparation during the last decade.) The 1982 survey was carried out by interviewing one person of at least sixteen years of age in each of approximately 11,000 households in England and Wales. A further 5,000 households in Scotland were also included in the survey. The respondents chosen for the survey, with the electoral register used as a sampling frame, were all given the main 'screening' questionnaire by interviewers. This enabled the collection of background information about respondents in addition to establishing whether they, or other members of their household, had been a victim of crime within the previous fourteen months. Obviously the survey did not attempt to include offences which cannot easily be incorporated into research of this type, that is, where there is no obvious or individual victim. The offences which were included in the survey were divided into 'personal' offences, such as thefts from the person, robberies, assaults and sexual offences, and 'household' offences, such as burglary, vandalism, and car-related crime. Respondents were questioned about their own experience in relation to personal offences, but were also asked more generally about events affecting any member of their household in relation to household offences. In asking respondents about particular types of crime, care was taken to paraphrase the legal definition of the offence so as to make its ambit more easily understood by respondents.[11]

Where the respondent indicated that he or she had been a victim of a personal offence, or that a household offence had been committed against themselves or another household member, a 'victim form' was completed to give details of the offence or offences which had occurred during the relevant period. These details included the location of the offence, how it happened, whether it was reported and what (if anything) was known about the offender. The final stage of the survey was conducted by giving a third (or 'follow-up') questionnaire to all victims and a sample of non-victims. This additional questionnaire was concerned with gathering information about the respondents' lifestyles and whether this had any bearing on their likelihood of victimization. It also dealt with respondents' fears of and attitudes to crime, their dealings with the police, and their own conduct.

Although it is not possible to set out all of the first BCS findings here, it is worth looking in detail at some of the results.[12] In relation to the BCS estimates for the number of incidents in England and Wales coming within the offence categories covered by the survey, it should be remembered that they were derived from a sample and cannot hope to be any more than an approximation. Nevertheless, it is interesting to compare the BCS estimates with the crimes recorded by the police, in the comparable offence categories, for the same period (that is, 1981). The BCS, not surprisingly, revealed that many more incidents occurred than were recorded in the police statistics, although a large number of these incidents were relatively trivial in nature. The survey suggested that there were

> twice as many burglaries as were recorded by the police; nearly five times as much wounding; twelve times as much theft from the person; and thirteen times as much vandalism (or criminal damage). Taking crimes of violence together (sexual offences, robbery and wounding), there were on the basis of survey estimates five times as many incidents as were recorded; for incidents involving loss of or damage to property the figure was four times. The overall ratio for incidents which had been compared was one in four.[13]

Only in relation to car theft did the estimates from the BCS suggest a similar rate of offending as the official statistics. This is probably explained by the fact that victims of this offence will need to enlist the help of the police to recover their vehicle and will, in any case, be obliged to report the incident for insurance purposes. Elsewhere, the rate of reporting incidents (or recording them) was fairly low, with the lowest reporting rates being in respect of vandalism and theft in a dwelling. The following table is derived from BCS data and shows the percentage of BCS offences reported to the police, for each category, in descending order.

Table 3.1 *Source: BCS*

Offence category	Percentage reported
Theft of motor vehicle	95
Burglary	66
Bicycle theft	64
Robbery	47
Wounding	39
Theft from the person	31
Theft from motor vehicle	30
Sexual offences	28
Vandalism	22
Theft in a dwelling	18

Victims who did not report an incident to the police were asked for their reasons for not doing so. The triviality of the incident (or that it caused no loss or damage) was by far the most common reason for non-reporting. The belief that the police could be of little assistance was another commonly occurring reason for not reporting an incident, especially in relation to offences such as vandalism. The only other fairly frequent reason given for non-reporting (i.e. in 13 per cent of personal offences where the police were not notified), was that some victims of violent offences felt that the incidents were not appropriate for police involvement. It was interesting that certain reasons – such as dislike of the police – which were often thought to be associated with non-reporting, were rarely given by victims. However, it did emerge that victims who had a more favourable attitude towards the police in general were more likely to report relatively trivial incidents than those with a less favourable impression.

Although a considerable proportion of unreported incidents could be categorized as 'less serious' ones, it would be erroneous to think that the dark figure of crime is made up largely of trivial offences. The BCS also revealed quite a number of more serious incidents which were not reported to the police by the victims. In relation to theft of property worth between £100 and £250 (in 1981), a third of all incidents were not reported. A sizeable number of violent incidents which caused some injury to the victim also went unreported.

The BCS also drew comparisons, albeit tentatively, with the results of major crime surveys in other countries. The burglary rate in the United States was estimated as twice as high as in Britain, and the burglary rate in Canada was also thought to exceed our own.[14] Robbery was also more common in the United States and Canada than in Britain, on the evidence of victimization surveys, but car theft was more of a problem in Britain than in North America.

In relation to specific offences, the BCS findings were of considerable value in identifying those most at risk of victimization. For robbery, very few offences were revealed by the survey, so any conclusions must be treated with caution. However, from the available evidence, it appeared that those most at risk were young men living in heavily populated or inner-city areas, especially those who often went out in the evenings. The popular image of the stereotypical elderly (or elderly female) victim of robbery or 'mugging' was not, therefore, supported by the BCS findings. In relation to burglary, it was once again found that living in an inner-city area greatly increased the risk of victimization. Respondents living in houses were found to be safer than those in flats, and owner-occupiers were safer than those living in council properties. Not surprisingly, those households where no one was at home for large portions of the day were more at risk than those which were continuously occupied.

The BCS estimated that the combined figure for vehicle theft, theft from vehicles, and vandalism to vehicles represented around one third of all property offences which were disclosed during the survey. In relation to theft of or from cars, those living in inner-city areas, especially those who were not able to garage their vehicles, were found to be most at risk of victimization. The vulnerability of cars and their contents clearly has implications for crime prevention initiatives, and the security industry, as well as for urban planning.

The BCS found that serious assaults were rare occurrences. But taking all types of assault together, for the purposes of assessing those most at risk, it was found that chances of victimization were higher for men, the under-thirties, the unmarried, those who went out frequently in the evening (especially 'drinkers'), and those who themselves were prone to use violence on others. Once again, contrary to the media stereotypes of victims of violence, it was neither old people nor women who were found to be most at risk. Interestingly, the chance of being assaulted was as high away from the cities as it was in the inner-city areas. To a large extent, the characteristics of the offender were similar to those of the victim, in that they were likely to be young men who went out a lot, especially to pubs. It is also significant that quite a large proportion of victims – around one third – knew their attackers. (Quite commonly the offender was a husband, relative or ex-partner of the victim.)

A relatively small proportion of victims of violence were found to be women. But it is a strong possibility, judging from other research, that the BCS was not a very suitable method for uncovering this type of offence. The nature of a household interview with a strange person is hardly conducive to a respondent revealing that she has been raped, or indecently assaulted, or attacked by a husband or partner. There may well be some other member of the household present at the time of the interview and the respondent may not reveal an incident, either through embarrassment or even fear of reprisals.

Because fear of crime was perceived as a serious problem in its own right, the BCS also asked questions to gauge the level of anxiety of respondents about being a victim of either crimes of violence or property offences. It should be noted, however, that where victimization surveys deal with respondents' attitudes (as opposed to events) it is not advisable to treat the results as 'facts', as it is questionable how accurately such matters as fear of crime can be meaningfully measured. Drawing upon the experience of North American surveys, the BCS asked all respondents about how safe they felt when walking alone after dark in their area. It was found that women were more fearful than men and that age was also an important factor, with older respondents (especially older women) being the most fearful group. Respondents living in inner-city areas were more anxious about being attacked than those living in other areas. In inner-city areas, over half of the female respondents (and 58 per cent of elderly women) said that their fear for personal safety made them reluctant to walk through their neighbourhood after dark.

In addition, the survey asked respondents how worried were they that they, or some other family member, might become a victim of crime. Once again, those most fearful of personally becoming victims were women, the elderly and those living in inner-city areas. But, in relation to anxiety about the safety of other members of their household, respondents with families and children tended to be more fearful. Forty per cent of respondents claimed not to worry about crime at all, but those who did worry were asked about the crimes which troubled them most. It emerged that burglary caused the most anxiety, followed (in descending order) by mugging, sexual assault, assault, vandalism and car theft.[15]

It is both interesting and ironic that those people who tend to be most fearful of becoming a victim of crimes such as robbery or assault in public places are also those who appear to be least likely actually to become victims of such crimes. Of course, 'lifestyle' may play an important part in either increasing or decreasing one's risk of victimization; a person who rarely goes out for fear of being attacked, is less likely to be attacked. But even allowing for this possibility, it seems that much fear of 'street crime' is misplaced. On the other hand, most of our fears are hardly based on actuarial prediction and rational assessment! It should also be borne in mind that fear of (say) assault is perhaps not just based on the *likelihood* of it happening, but on the *consequences* if it does occur. For this reason it is hardly surprising that the elderly are more fearful than the young, and that women are more anxious than men. It should be appreciated that male respondents are probably less willing to reveal their fears to an interviewer than their female counterparts.[16]

In an effort to gain a more detailed picture of respondents' attitudes to different aspects of the criminal justice system, victims were asked how they thought 'their' offender (if caught) deserved to be dealt with for the offence. The BCS found that victims were not, on the whole, particularly punitive-minded, with only 10 per cent advocating a custodial sentence for their offender. Around half did not think that a court appearance was appropriate for their offender, and where a court sentence was thought to be desirable, a fine was the most commonly chosen penalty. About 15 per cent made some reference to reparation by the offender either to society (for example, in the form of community service) or to the victim (by the payment of compensation). Although these findings must be interpreted with some caution, they are nevertheless of considerable interest. On the one hand, they illustrate the fact that many of the incidents uncovered by the BCS were comparatively minor and therefore the appropriate response by the criminal justice system should not always be punitive. But on the other, these results suggest that even where punishment is thought necessary, the general public are perhaps not so keen to see a hard-line approach pursued by the courts as we are sometimes led to believe, especially by certain sections of the media.[17]

The BCS found that only one in five victims whose incidents brought them into contact with the police were dissatisfied with police performance. Older victims tended to be more satisfied with police performance than younger ones. Where there was any dissatisfaction, it was more likely to be for lack of action by the police than for any other reason (such as an unsympathetic attitude by the police). Similarly, where respondents had approached the police for assistance for any other reason, there was generally a high level of satisfaction with police behaviour. However, young men, especially in inner cities, were far less likely to be happy with the police response to their requests for help. Generally, the BCS found that the police needed to ensure that the support of the young was encouraged and improved.[18]

The great value of victimization research was amply demonstrated by this initial 'sweep' of the BCS in 1982. It shed light on the dark figure of unreported and unrecorded crime, it helped identify those most at risk of victimization (for the offence categories covered), and it assessed the effects of crime on victims. In addition, it investigated the extent of fear of crime as a distinct social problem and provided useful information about public attitudes to police performance and to sentencing practice. In revealing a large quantity of unreported crime, the BCS suggested that rises in official crime figures should not be interpreted too literally. For example, a relatively modest increase in the rate of reporting incidents by the public could give a misleading impression of a large increase in crime. The survey also indicated that although increasing the manpower of the police is no guarantee of effectively preventing or detecting crime, a good deal can be done to help educate the public in crime prevention and the need for greater security. It will be remembered that the motor car was the most common target of property offences disclosed to the BCS and a great deal could be done to reduce the opportunity offered to would-be thieves and vandals.

Victimization surveys increase in value by repetition as greater confidence can be placed in their estimates for the total number of offences committed in each offence category. Also, successive sweeps of a national survey offer an opportunity to gauge the growth of crime (if any) over a specific period, in contrast to the growth in official or recorded crime. For these reasons, the BCS has been repeated in the same basic form, but with suitable modifications and additions, in 1984, 1988, 1992, 1994 and 1996. It is not intended to provide such a detailed analysis of the 1984 and 1988 surveys, but the 1992 sweep in the series will be looked at more closely, as it enables us to monitor the extent and growth of crime over a ten-year period of research. Finally, the 1994 sweep, and its innovative methodology, will be considered briefly.

The second BCS sweep also took a sample of around 11,000 in England and Wales, using the electoral register as a sampling frame. This time there was no Scottish sample. The central or 'core' questions about victimization in relation to specific offences and about the details of incidents, remained the same, but some changes were introduced in relation to the less central issues.[19] The fieldwork for the second survey was carried out by NOP Market Research (a task which this company also performed for the Aberystwyth Crime Survey in 1993). The same three-stage process was used as in 1982; that is, a screening questionnaire, the collection of details of incidents on victim forms, and a follow-up questionnaire for all victims and two-fifths of non-victims.

The second survey found that property offences were much more common than offences of violence (with wounding, robbery and sexual offences together making up just 5 per cent of all incidents). As with the first sweep of the survey, vehicles were particularly vulnerable and one third of all incidents disclosed to the 1984 survey related to either damage to vehicles, or to thefts of or from them.[20] Once again, vehicle theft was the only offence category for which there was a very high rate of reporting of incidents. For some types of theft, and for vandalism, only about 20 per cent of incidents were reported to the police and there was also a low rate of reporting for assaults (about one third). Burglaries were more commonly reported, with around two-thirds being brought to the attention of the police. As with the first sweep, the second survey suggested that a considerable number of incidents reported to the police do not get recorded as crime.

The second BCS survey estimated that between 1981 and 1983, for those offence categories which could be compared with police statistics, there had been a 10 per cent increase in the number of household offences, with a smaller increase in all personal offences. For the same period, police statistics showed a 12 per cent increase in recorded crime for the comparable offence categories. By itself, this finding was far from conclusive, but it might well have indicated that certain crimes were being more commonly reported to the police, and hence the larger growth in crime reflected in the official figures. When BCS estimates for burglary were combined with those from the General Household Survey (which was repeated throughout the 1970s), the findings were rather more conclusive. In the period between 1972 and 1983, recorded burglaries doubled in number, but in contrast, the GHS and BCS estimates suggest a much more modest rise of around 29 per cent. What appears to have happened is that many more burglaries were being reported to the police and, in turn, recorded by them; but the increase in the burglary rate was actually much less dramatic than the official figures seemed to indicate.[21]

The second BCS asked victims to rate the seriousness of 'their' offence on a 0–20 scale with the upper end being the most serious. It was found that, in general, the offence categories which were more highly rated on this scale tended to be those which were more frequently reported to the police. These offences included car theft, burglary, wounding and robbery. Conversely, offences rated as less serious tended to have low reporting rates; but sexual offences were rated highly in terms of seriousness and still had a low rate of reporting.[22]

The survey also found that people appeared to be more willing to report property offences if they had a favourable impression of the police, and manual workers were generally less likely to notify the police of such offences. It is true that manual workers tended to be less favourably disposed towards the police, in terms of their performance, but there may also have been other reasons for a lower rate of reporting than for their non-manual counterparts. For example, non-manual victims of property crime were more likely to be insured and thus more likely to report incidents. The survey also suggested that young people were less inclined to notify the police of offences committed against them than were older victims. Again, a less favourable perception of the police may have been one (but not the sole) reason for this finding.

As part of its inquiry into the impact of crime on victims, both financially and emotionally, the second BCS also included questions about victim support schemes so as to help evaluate their effectiveness. Very few victims uncovered by the survey were offered help by a victim support scheme, although a much larger number stated that they had heard of the scheme and thought that it was a good idea. Of course, not all of those who favoured these schemes in general thought that assistance from a victim support volunteer would have been appropriate in their own particular case. Of those victims who would have welcomed assistance from such a scheme, it tended to be respondents who were most affected by the incident, notably as a result of crimes such as robbery and burglary.

The second sweep of the survey elicited a similar response to the first in relation to respondents' fear for personal safety, with women, the elderly and inner-city residents feeling least safe. The survey also asked about fear of specific crimes such as burglary, robbery and rape.[23] It was found that 30 per cent of female respondents were 'very worried' about being a victim of rape and, for the youngest age group (16–30 years old), 41 per cent were very worried. Rape was a very rare occurrence in the offences uncovered by the BCS, but it should not be forgotten that many rapes and sexual assaults go unreported. It is also fair to say that fear is not necessarily based on any statistical probability of actually being victimized, as it will be the consequences of an offence rather than the likelihood of it happening which may instil fear into respondents' minds.

The second BCS asked respondents about their attitude to Neighbourhood or Home Watch schemes. These schemes have proliferated since the time of this survey but it is nonetheless surprising that less than 1 per cent of respondents participated in such a home watch scheme at this time. However, nearly two-thirds of the sample indicated that they would be willing to join a scheme in their neighbourhood. Of those who evinced no willingness to participate, a variety of reasons were given for this reticence. These included the respondents' lifestyle (too busy or often away from home), age or health, or their doubts about the efficacy of these schemes in general.

The 1988 BCS

The third sweep of the BCS took place in 1988 and some of its findings may be briefly noted. Once again, the BCS used the electoral register to provide its core sample and, as in 1982, a Scottish sample of 5,000 was also included in the survey. But there was a difference in the England and Wales sample from the previous sweeps. In addition to one adult aged sixteen or over in each of 10,392 households being interviewed (the core sample), there was also a second, ethnic minority (booster) sample of 1,349 respondents. The latter sample, comprising both Afro-Caribbean and Asian people, was included so as to study the rate of victimization amongst racial minority groups and also to examine their attitudes towards the police. (This sample was not derived from the electoral register.) The survey once again used a main screening questionnaire, and victim forms to record details of incidents which were revealed to interviewers. Follow-up questionnaires were then used (in two different versions) to gather information about crime prevention and security measures in one version, and about attitudes to and experience of the police in the other.

As with earlier sweeps, the 1988 survey found that the overwhelming majority of incidents related to property offences. Cars were once again found to be particularly vulnerable with around one third of incidents disclosed to the survey relating to motor vehicles (i.e. thefts of or from them, or vandalism to them). Over half of all incidents involved some form of theft; burglaries represented around 9 per cent, and common assaults about 11 per cent of all BCS incidents. More serious crimes of violence were less common (6 per cent), but as with previous surveys there is a strong possibility that many sexual offences and acts of 'domestic' violence were not revealed to interviewers. The 1988 survey found that although car theft had a high reporting rate by victims, most other offences frequently were not reported to the police. Incidents involving vandalism and theft had low reporting rates, and so too did sexual offences and incidents involving wounding. Burglaries were more frequently reported by victims (that is, in nearly two-thirds of incidents), especially where some loss was incurred.[24]

One of the big advantages of a continuing crime survey programme is that it enables comparisons to be made, over time, and provides some indication of any growth or decline in the crime rate for those offences which are covered by the surveys. In comparing figures obtained from the first three sweeps of the survey, it was found that household offences as a whole increased by 29 per cent between 1981 and 1987. In contrast, during the same period, personal offences increased by only 7 per cent. Where comparisons with police statistics were possible, it was found that whereas recorded crime rose by 41 per cent (in the 1981–7 period), there was only a 30 per cent increase in BCS offences. A likely explanation of these figures is that although crime increased during this six-year period, a growing willingness on the part of victims to report incidents to the police led to a bigger growth in 'official' or recorded crime than actually occurred. The 1988 BCS revealed a 15 per cent increase in reporting since 1981 for crimes which were comparable to those recorded by the police.[25] It could be argued that this growing willingness to report incidents suggests that the crimes suffered by victims are becoming more serious in nature. However, the BCS found little evidence to support this contention, and it appears more likely that higher reporting rates reflect a change in public attitudes to certain types of crime (including petty crime) and greater publicity given to crime prevention schemes in general. The same six-year period also witnessed a growth in owner-occupier households and access to a telephone; these two factors may have influenced the reporting rate of incidents.

It is particularly interesting to compare the official figures for burglary with loss with those estimates derived from the BCS and the General Household Survey combined (permitting a comparison over a fifteen-year period). Whilst the crime survey estimates suggest a modest rise of 17 per cent in such incidents between 1972 and 1987, police figures indicate a massive 127 per cent increase. How can this discrepancy be explained? It would seem that more victims are now reporting burglaries and that this may also have something to do with the fact that many more households were insured for such loss in 1987 than they were fifteen years earlier. Another explanatory factor is that there is evidence that the police were more likely to record burglary incidents reported to them than they were fifteen years earlier. The combined BCS and GHS estimates suggest that whilst 59 per cent of burglaries reported to the police were recorded by them in 1972, this figure had risen to 85 per cent by 1987. These estimates (and they are only estimates) suggest that there was not, in fact, a massive increase in burglary during the 1970s and the 1980s. Instead, there was a considerable change in reporting and recording trends accompanied by a more modest growth in incidents.

As with earlier sweeps, the 1988 survey found that the most common reason for not reporting an offence was that the victim felt that it was too trivial or that it caused no damage or loss. The next most frequent explanation given for non-reporting was that the victim thought that the police would have been unable to do anything constructive even if informed. Although the survey found once again that fear or dislike of the police was not a common reason for failure to report an offence, there was some evidence that the public were now more likely to feel that the police would not be interested in the incident in question. Comparing the 1988 findings with those of 1984, it also seemed that victims were becoming less satisfied with the way in which the police handled the matter when they *were* informed of an offence. This trend was consistent for nearly all offence categories, so it is hard to ignore the decline in levels of satisfaction with the efforts made by the police. However, it may well be that even in this relatively short period, the public's expectations of the police had increased.

The 1988 survey disclosed little difference in the reporting rates between white victims, and Asian and Afro-Caribbean victims. (It will be remembered that this sweep included a booster sample which facilitated these comparisons.) Although it appeared that ethnic minority victims were more likely to report burglary and vandalism to the home, this could be due to the fact that they suffered greater loss and damage as a result of incidents and, in turn, this may have affected the reporting rate. The survey did find a marked difference in levels of satisfaction with the police when an offence was reported. Whereas around 60 per cent of white victims were satisfied (either very or fairly) with the police response, only around half of Afro-Caribbeans shared this satisfaction, and Asian victims were even less satisfied (only 44 per cent). Ethnic minority victims were more critical of the effort made by the police in response to their report of an incident, and Afro-Caribbean victims were more likely than other respondents to complain of the police attitude (for example, impoliteness) towards them.[26]

A novel feature of the 1988 sweep of the survey was the inclusion of questions sponsored by the Health and Safety Executive Committee on Violence, about victimization at work. Some questions were asked to assess the frequency of workers suffering verbal abuse by members of the public (not colleagues). As this is such a subjective experience and one in which the respondent may have been equally culpable, it must be doubted how useful the findings are. Also, unlike most of the criminal incidents covered by the survey, experience of verbal abuse may easily be forgotten or distorted. But, for what it is worth, the survey found that around 14 per cent of workers experienced verbal abuse at work from a member of the public during the survey period. Rates of victimization were higher amongst young workers, especially young women. Whether this was due to the greater propensity of this age group to be abusive in return is difficult to judge. All that can be certain is that such figures should be treated with some caution. The survey found no evidence of Afro-Caribbean workers suffering more abuse than white counterparts, although Asian workers appeared to be victimized slightly more frequently.

Respondents' places of work were found to be the location where much victimization occurred, especially in relation to theft and assault. But as working people spend a considerable proportion of their day at their place of employment this is hardly surprising, particularly when work brings many people into close contact with fellow employees and offers much scope for criminal incidents. However, the survey was also interested to study 'job-related' crime: that is, whether the nature of a particular job increased the likelihood of certain types of victimization. The survey looked at three particular offence categories – violence, threats, and thefts, and working respondents were asked whether the incident happened 'because of the nature of [their] job'. It was found that working respondents thought that almost a quarter of violent incidents that they suffered were job-related, and slightly more than a quarter of personal thefts. A little over a third of threats made to working respondents were also assessed by them as job-related The public were much more likely than colleagues to be blamed by working respondents for the violent incidents which they suffered and for threats. In relation to job-related thefts, however, workers blamed the public for only half of these incidents.

The survey suggested that people who worked in education, health and welfare occupations were particularly at risk of being threatened or assaulted. Welfare workers and female nurses were particularly susceptible to being attacked, as were female office managers, managers of pubs, and security men. Teachers, social workers, nurses, pub managers, and security workers were more likely than other occupational groups to experience threats. In interpreting these findings, it should be borne in mind that different occupational groups may have different views on what constitutes an assault or a threat. In other words, some people are more sensitive than others to certain incidents and the more educated (or higher status) the respondents, the more likely it may be that they will categorize an incident as a threat or an assault. But, nevertheless, the possibility of 'response bias' cannot undermine the main thrust of the survey's findings about those occupational groups which are most at risk of job-related crime.[27]

The 1988 survey was of particular interest as it included a booster sample of around 700 Afro-Caribbean respondents and nearly 1,000 Asian people. It was found that, overall, these two ethnic minority groups had higher rates of victimization than white people. (Of course, other explanatory variables, such as the areas in which respondents lived and their social position, may have significantly influenced the respective rates of victimization). Afro-Caribbeans were more vulnerable to burglary than Asians or whites, and they were also more likely to be victims of assault than either of the other two groups. Asians shared with Afro-Caribbeans a significantly higher rate of victimization (than whites) for threats, robbery and theft from the person. Asian respondents were also more likely to experience vandalism than the other groups.[28]

The BCS attempted to assess whether ethnic origin alone could account for higher victimization rates for Afro-Caribbeans and Asians. This was done by taking account of other variables which are associated with higher risk, by means of 'multivariate' analysis. It was found, for example, that the apparent vulnerability of Asian respondents to threats was probably more a consequence of where they lived, their age and social class than their ethnic origin. On the other hand, higher rates of vandalism against Asian people seemed to be racially motivated. There was little evidence that ethnic differences alone could explain the higher rates of victimization for Afro-Caribbeans compared to white respondents. For example, once age, residence, family and other social factors were taken into account, Afro-Caribbeans were not significantly more likely to be victims of burglary. This is not to suggest that ethnic minorities are not more likely to be victims of offences; it is merely to point out that demographic factors may well play an important part in this. It is certainly not to deny that many incidents *are* racially motivated and that victims may well feel that this is the case, even in instances when it is not. Moreover, it was found that victims from the ethnic minority groups were likely to suffer offences of greater seriousness than their white counterparts.[29] It should also be stated that, to the victim, it is little consolation to think that the crime occurred more as a result of where he or she lived than because of their ethnicity; the consequences of the incident may well be the same.

The 1988 survey found that respondents were much more aware of neighbourhood watch schemes than the 1984 sample. There was also increased membership of such schemes and, of those who were not members, two-thirds were interested in joining a scheme if one were established in their area. Of those respondents who were members of a scheme, there was quite a high rate of satisfaction with them. The perceived benefits of membership included a feeling of greater security, deterring crime, and an increased awareness of the risks of victimization. Some respondents (albeit a small number) thought that the existence of the home watch scheme improved the community spirit of their area.

The 1992 Survey

The next sweep of the BCS was conducted in 1992, allowing patterns of crime and reporting trends now to be studied over a ten-year period (1981–91) since the first survey. The 1992 survey took a core sample of around 10,000 households in England and Wales. Like the previous sweep, there was also a further booster sample of Afro-Caribbeans and Asians. (In addition, there was also a sample of children of between twelve and fifteen years who lived in households which were included in the other two samples). A departure from previous practice was the use of the Postcode Address File as a sampling frame instead of the electoral register, as it was felt that this would produce a better coverage of all household addresses in the country. The three-stage questionnaire method (i.e. 'main', 'victim form', and 'follow-up') was once again used in the survey.

The survey found that 'vehicle crime' made up 36 per cent of offences disclosed; this category includes vandalism to vehicles, theft of vehicles, and theft (or attempted theft) from vehicles. Violent crime represented just over 5 per cent, with common assault making up a further 12 per cent. The other categories were burglary (11 per cent), home vandalism (7 per cent), other thefts (27 per cent), and theft from the person (3 per cent). Clearly, offences against property, especially the motor car, were by far the most common. Violent crime by comparison occurred much less frequently.

Once again, it was found that vehicle theft had the highest reporting rate (99 per cent) by victims. This is not surprising, as victims know that notifying the police is the most likely method of recovering their cars and that any insurance claim would require this action to have been taken. Burglary with loss also had a high reporting rate (92 per cent), as did bicycle theft (69 per cent) to a slightly lesser extent. The percentage reporting rates for the other offence categories were: burglary without loss (53), theft from vehicles (53), robbery (41), wounding (48), attempted theft of vehicles (41), other personal theft (38), theft from the person (36), vandalism to vehicles (31), other household theft (29), common assault (26), and household vandalism (25). In view of the seriousness of such crimes, it is surprising that slightly under half of all robbery and wounding offences were reported to the police. Of course, not all reported incidents were recorded by the police as offences. Where comparisons were possible between BCS incidents and police statistics, it was found that slightly less than two-thirds of reported offences were recorded by the police. This means that, overall, only around 30 per cent of incidents were included in police records for the comparable offence categories.

Looking at reporting trends throughout the first ten years of the BCS programme, it seems that more incidents are now being reported by victims than a decade earlier. In 1981, only 31 per cent of all BCS incidents were reported to the police, whereas ten years later 43 per cent were reported.[30] For those incidents which can be compared to recorded offence categories, the reporting rate has risen from 36 to 50 per cent over the same ten-year period. These trends suggest that more incidents are now being brought to the attention of the police and that there is now a smaller dark figure of unreported and unrecorded crime.

For these reasons, it is prudent not to take the large growth in official crime figures at face value. An upward trend in reporting by the public might easily give the impression of a crime wave, when in reality the growth in crime might have been much more modest. But there is some concern that if victims are now reporting crime more readily to the police, the nature of incidents may have increased in seriousness over this ten-year period. After all, offence seriousness has been shown to be an important determinant of whether an incident will be reported by a victim. It is difficult to assess whether victims are now suffering more serious offences, and the findings from the BCS cannot be conclusive for methodological reasons.[31] It is perhaps more likely that the tolerance of victims is lower today and that they are less likely to put up with criminal incidents or other anti-social behaviour. The greater prominence given to crime prevention and to notifying the police of incidents may have contributed to an increase in the reporting rate. So too may the growth in both owner-occupation of property and access to a telephone. Another influential factor is the fact that many more victims today are insured against loss or damage to their property.[32]

For BCS offences which can be compared with official or recorded offences, it was found that the growth in BCS estimates (1981–91) has been less dramatic than the rise in recorded crime. Whilst recorded offences increased by 96 per cent during this period, incidents disclosed to the BCS increased by 49 per cent. However, the number of BCS incidents which were reported to the police during this period rose at a rate which was broadly in line with the growth in official crime reflected in police statistics. In relation to wounding and robbery, BCS estimates suggest a relatively modest increase of around 20 per cent during the ten-year period, whereas recorded offences have risen by around 80 per cent. As well as reflecting an increase in both reporting and recording of violent incidents, the official figures may also be a result of greater attention now being paid by the police to domestic and other types of violence. For example, the police may have become more willing to classify certain types of assault as 'wounding' than previously.

As with previous sweeps of the survey, the most common reason (given by 55 per cent) for not reporting an incident was its triviality or the fact that no tangible loss resulted. The next most frequent reason (given by 25 per cent) was the belief that the police could not do anything about the incident. The proportion of 'non-reporters' (13 per cent) who felt that the police would not be interested is worthy of comment. This reason was given by only 7 per cent of non-reporters in 1984, and by 10 per cent in 1988. It seems that a feeling has grown amongst victims, rightly or wrongly, that the police will be uninterested in their incident. However, it should be noted that fear or dislike of the police is rarely given as a reason for not reporting.

It is also possible to chart, over a period of time, the level of satisfaction of victims with the police response to their incident report. Although the 1992 survey found that a higher proportion were 'very satisfied' than in 1988 (29 per cent as compared with 22 per cent four years earlier), this was still a smaller proportion than in 1984 (31 per cent). The biggest increases in satisfaction with the police response between the 1988 and 1992 surveys were in relation to burglary, household theft, vandalism and robbery. The recent improvement in police response (as perceived by BCS victims) is consistent with the prominence which was given by the police and the Home Office, during this period, to improving communication with victims and providing a better service to them.[33] However, the more favourable impression that the police have made on BCS victims over the last few years, is not reflected in the general perception of BCS respondents of the police. The proportion of all respondents (i.e. victims and non-victims) who thought that their local police did a very good job declined from 25 per cent in 1988 to 24 per cent in 1992. (This is appreciably lower than 34 per cent in 1984.)

We have already considered the general growth in crime during the last decade as reflected (differently) in both the BCS and police figures.

In relation to burglaries with loss it is possible to compare the estimates for the BCS and the General Household Survey, which together go back to 1972, with the recorded statistics for this offence over the same twenty-year period. Survey estimates (for the BCS and GHS) show a 61 per cent increase in this time, whilst police statistics have increased by 189 per cent.[34] As we have seen, this large discrepancy may be partly explained by the increased tendency of victims of burglaries to report offences, and the reasons for this were discussed earlier. The BCS considered the factors which increase the risk of being a burglary victim, and inner-city households were found to be particularly vulnerable.[35] Other factors which appeared to be associated with higher risk were: living in flats or bedsits; living in a household where there is only one adult; and being out of the household for a large proportion of the time.[36]

There is a growing interest in the phenomenon of multiple or 'repeat' victimization.[37] This is because it has been shown that, for many types of offence, a person's chances of being victimized are considerably greater if he or she has previously been a victim of that offence.[38] The 1992 BCS found that households which had been burgled in the four years prior to 1991 were more than twice as likely to be burgled in 1991 than those households which had not been burgled during the previous four-year period. (This finding has obvious implications for crime prevention initiatives.) It was also found that 18 per cent of victims suffered more than one burglary incident over the fourteen-month recall period.[39] It could be argued that if a household is in a high-risk area or has other characteristics that make it more prone to burglary victimization, this could explain why it was the subject of multiple victimization. However, this can hardly explain why *particular* households (as opposed to others with roughly similar characteristics) appear to be more unfortunate than others. It would seem that certain households are picked out (possibly by the same offenders) *because* they have been burgled on an earlier occasion. The offenders may have found it an easy or vulnerable target, or they may have known that previously stolen items will have been replaced by new ones. It is also possible that one offender may have told another about the ease with which he burgled a particular household and the second offender may carry out a 'copy-cat' offence.[40]

The 1992 survey also looked closely at theft of and from vehicles. These offences (and attempts to commit them) made up around one quarter of all BCS incidents in this sweep. The factors most associated with risk of this type of victimization appeared to be: living in an inner-city area; having no garage and using street parking at night; living in flats or terraced houses (with no garage); and being affluent. Once again, the phenomenon of repeat victimization was evident. If a respondent had suffered the theft of his car in the four years prior to the survey period, his chances of being a victim of this crime during the survey period were greatly enhanced.

Repeat victimization was found to be particularly common in respect of violent offences,[41] with an estimated one third of victims of violence in 1991 experiencing more than one incident. It was also found that 17 per cent of violence victims experienced three or more incidents during the recall period. Whilst mugging offences are less likely to be repeated against the same victim, domestic violence against women is particularly likely to be inflicted on more than one occasion during the recall period. In looking at who commits these acts of violence, the survey found that in over half of all incidents the offender was known (if only by sight) to the victim. In a smaller, but still significant, proportion of cases the offender was well known to the victim. In only 43 per cent of all cases was the assailant a total stranger; these were more likely to be muggings or street offences. Not surprisingly, the survey found that most violence was inflicted by men. Very few offences (against adults) were committed by those aged under sixteen; the majority of assailants were thought to be in the 16–25 age range. But where violence occurred between people who were well known to one another, the offender was often older. For example, 57 per cent of domestic violence offenders were over twenty-five years of age.[42]

Whilst some types of violence, such as mugging, street crime and pub fights, have shown little change in number between 1981 and 1991, domestic and work-based assaults have shown a considerable increase. This might be attributable to a change in attitude and response to such incidents. Victims of domestic violence, for example, may now be more prepared to reveal offences to BCS interviewers. They may also be more willing to report such incidents to the police, but the evidence on this from successive sweeps of the survey is equivocal. Reporting of domestic violence increased considerably in the 1988 survey, but the rate had fallen back to earlier levels by 1992.

The findings from successive sweeps of the BCS have amply justified the investment of time and resources in this research programme. We considered earlier the potential benefits of this type of survey, and some of these (and several others besides) have been illustrated by the results of the BCS. Of course, there have been criticisms of the general orientation of the BCS programme, but before considering these in the next chapter it is worth noting the most recent BCS developments. Findings from the 1996 survey have not yet been published, but a brief synopsis of the 1994 results can be given here.[43]

The 1994 Survey

The 1994 survey took a larger main sample (14,500 people aged sixteen or over) than the earlier sweeps. The fieldwork, which was carried out by OPCS, made use of computer-assisted personal interviewing (CAPI). This method enables interviewers to use laptop computers to enter responses, and the questionnaire takes the form of a computer programme. This programme gives the questions, the range of possible answers, and the selection procedures to be followed in the interview. Although there are some drawbacks in using this system, there are also potential advantages for the future development of BCS surveys.[44] A particular value of CAPI in the 1994 sweep was that it enabled the computer to be 'turned round' for certain sensitive questions; this allowed respondents to read questions directly from the screen and to 'key in' their own answers (known as self-keying). Self-keying was used for three types of questions: in relation to self-reported drug use; handling stolen goods; and for women's experience of sexual victimization since the age of sixteen.

This was the first time that the questions relating to being offered, or buying, stolen goods have been asked by the BCS; 11 per cent said that they had bought something they believed to be stolen during the last five years. It is not possible to compare this figure with previous BCS findings. However, some comparison was possible for the questions about sexual assault during the last year and the earlier BCS questions on this subject. The 1994 survey disclosed much higher rates of rape and attempted rape than earlier sweeps; for example, 2.2 per cent of young women (age 16–29) were victims of rape in the previous twelve months.[45] In relation to drug misuse questions, respondents were more willing to answer by self-keying than they were in 1992, when they were given a self-completion questionnaire which they completed and placed in a sealed envelope. The admission rates for these offences (e.g. cannabis use) were much higher in 1994, especially among the younger respondents.

As with earlier sweeps, the preponderance of offences revealed to the 1994 interviewers were against property:

> nearly one in five were incidents of vandalism, and nearly a third were incidents of theft. Of the total, 9 per cent were burglaries (including attempts), and 24 per cent were thefts involving vehicles (including attempts). Violent crime (wounding and robbery) accounted for 5 per cent of the total, but common assaults, involving little or no injury, made up another 12 per cent.[46]

For BCS offences which can be compared with police statistics, it seemed that police figures were nearly four times lower than BCS estimates; i.e. 3.1 million recorded crimes compared with 11.6 million BCS incidents. For all BCS offences, it was found that 41 per cent were reported. Once again, car theft and burglary had high reporting rates, whereas vandalism and theft from the person did not. The main reasons for non-reporting were either that victims felt that the incident was not sufficiently serious, or that the police would not be able to do anything. But many serious incidents continued to go unreported to the police. The 1994 survey also revealed that the recording rate (by the police) of reported offences continues to fall. An estimated 57 per cent of reported crimes in the comparable sub-set (i.e. those which can be compared with police figures) were recorded by the police in 1993. This can be compared with 60 per cent of reported crimes which were recorded in 1991. There appears to be a lower rate of recording of property offences since 1981.

The 1994 sweep enabled a comparison between the rise in crime as revealed to the BCS, and that reflected in police statistics for the comparable sub-set, during the 1981 to 1993 period. Whilst recorded offences rose by 111 per cent in this time, the BCS figures (whether reported or not) suggest a less pronounced increase of 77 per cent. However, it is interesting to note that in the same period the number of BCS offences which were *reported* increased by around 130 per cent. (The possible reasons for the rise in the proportion of offences which are reported to the police were considered earlier in this chapter.) In relation to the 1991–3 period, the rise in BCS offences was sharper than that for officially recorded crime. The 1994 survey showed an 18 per cent increase, in contrast to the 7 per cent rise in recorded crime. Moreover, this larger increase in BCS crimes was evident across a range of offence categories. These findings suggest that the reporting rate of offences has started to fall in the last few years. It may be that in areas most prone to crime, residents are less likely today to be covered by insurance.

As with earlier sweeps, the 1994 survey considered which groups were most at risk of victimization. It was found that those living in inner-city areas, flats or bedsits, council and rented accommodation, faced much higher risks of burglary and other property offences. Households in the North were also more at risk than other areas. Interestingly, single parent families are particularly susceptible to victimization, as are certain ethnic minority groups. Of course, this may partly reflect the fact that certain groups are more likely to live in the residential areas which are most vulnerable. In relation to 'contact' crimes, such as assault and robbery, it is young people (particularly men) who are most at risk. It appears that crime has risen more sharply outside inner-city areas in recent times; for example, those in the South (outside London), the West

Midlands and Wales have been exposed to a higher than average rise in crime.

The 1994 survey also looked at fear of crime and its findings have been analysed in a separate report.[47] Burglary continued to head the list of crimes about which respondents were 'very worried', closely followed by rape. Indeed, it appeared that more respondents were very worried about these offences than about the possibility of personal illness, being involved in a road accident, or losing their jobs. It was found that amongst car owners anxiety about car theft was even greater than worry about burglary. In view of the increase in car-related crime, it is not surprising that anxiety about this type of victimization has risen sharply since 1988. However, fear of burglary has risen only slightly during the last ten years and fear of mugging remained much the same as in 1984, with just a modest increase in the proportion of respondents who were very or fairly worried.

Elderly people felt less safe when out alone at night in their area, with elderly women easily the most anxious group of respondents. However, the elderly were less worried than other groups about burglary and car theft. Women were more anxious in relation to most offences, with the exception of theft from cars. It was suggested that women's fear of crime was not generally a result of fears about random attacks by strangers, but rather a realistic reflection of the types of victimization that many women suffer commonly at the hands of men; e.g. domestic violence, insulting comments, harassment at work, and being followed. It was also found that inner-city and less affluent residents were more fearful of crime and that Asian and Afro-Caribbean families were more anxious than white respondents.

4

Regional Crime Surveys

Introduction

We have seen how crime or victimization surveys can be used to shed light on the dark figure of unreported and unrecorded crime, and how the value of this research is not restricted to simply providing estimates of crime and victimization for the purpose of comparison with official statistics. Unlike police figures, victimization surveys are able to study the effects of crime and the social variables which are associated with a high risk of victimization. Moreover, they enable researchers to use the questionnaires to gather more subjective information in relation to respondents' fear of crime, views on the police and law enforcement, punishment and crime prevention.

So far, we have concentrated on the national programme of research, but it will be obvious that the same methodology can be used on a local or regional basis also. In looking at local surveys, it can be seen that their underlying ambit and purpose can vary. Some have used very similar methodology to the national survey, whilst others have been more overtly political in orientation, using the survey *inter alia* as part of a campaign for more locally accountable policing. This is not surprising in view of the fact that some local surveys have been funded, at least in part, by local councils. Of course, there is no 'correct' or proper use of victimization surveys – they can serve a variety of purposes. But the more political use of victimization research should be noted, and it has to be taken account of when assessing the various surveys which have been conducted during the last decade.[1] It is not proposed to review all of the regional surveys in this chapter, but a selection has been chosen which, one hopes, reflects a variety of areas, methodologies and purposes.

Manchester Survey of Female Victims (1986)

An interesting example of a local victim survey which contrasts totally with the academic or scientific approach of the British Crime Survey, is that conducted by Manchester City Council's Police Monitoring Unit. This Unit was predominantly concerned with issues of police accountability and civil liberties. Its outlook was overtly political and critical of police organization and practice. In its monthly publication, *Police Watch*, it included a questionnaire, for its women readers only, which asked them about fear of crime, and their experiences as victims (where appropriate) and whether or not they reported the incident(s). The article accompanying the questionnaire stated that 'violence against women, both in the home and on the streets, is given a very low priority by the police'.[2] Thus one of the questions which the survey was designed to ask was seemingly prejudged by this and other observations. The article also stated:

> Many women dare not go out alone after dark for fear of being assaulted. Others are beaten or raped in their own homes yet never turn to the police for help. In Manchester both individual women and women's organisations complain about the police being unsympathetic when dealing with women who have been assaulted, raped or sexually abused . . . In order to give many more women a say about policing we are carrying out this survey. We want to find out how you have been treated by police in Manchester and how you feel about your contacts with the police.[3]

Thus the questionnaire was not presented to readers in a 'value-free' context. Readers were, to some extent, primed with selected information and a number of sensational newspaper headlines which were interspersed amongst the questions. Respondents were not a random sample of the population. They were drawn from readers of *Police Watch* and, it might be argued, women were more likely to complete the questionnaire if they had some experience of crime to report. If they had no incident to report, or no antipathy towards the police, they were possibly less likely to complete and return the questionnaire. (Indeed, such women were unlikely to be readers of *Police Watch*!) The editors of *Police Watch* responded to criticisms that the survey was unscientific and that their findings were unrepresentative of women in Manchester generally, by arguing that they were 'not interested in making generalised statements or getting involved in discussions about the scientific validity of the information' derived from the questionnaires.[4]

Although the methodology used for the Manchester survey was seriously flawed, it will be remembered that the British Crime Survey provided comparatively little information about violent offences committed against women. For all its limitations, the Manchester survey represented an attempt to focus on female victims and to gather information about their experiences, both in relation to the crimes that they suffered and their contacts with the police. Replies were received from 1,841 women, and respondents were fairly evenly distributed throughout the different areas of the city. The age of respondents ranged from thirteen to ninety-seven; the average age was thirty-six. A wide range of occupations were represented by the survey's respondents, in addition to retired women, housewives, students and the unemployed. Respondents were asked about the type of accommodation they were living in: 42 per cent were owner-occupiers; 35 per cent rented from the council; 20 per cent rented from a private landlord; 1 per cent rented from a housing association and 1 per cent lived in a hostel. (This distribution was thought to be roughly in line with the general population in Manchester.) Women of Afro-Caribbean or Asian origin made up 5 per cent of the total number of respondents.

Respondents were asked if they had experienced particular crimes of violence or threatening behaviour. However, no time limit was put on this question – respondents were simply asked to specify (after each incident) how long ago it occurred. The survey found:

- 226 women reported sexual assault
- 152 women reported rape
- 311 women reported assault
- 43 women reported racial attack
- 587 women reported indecent exposure
- 648 women reported threatening or obscene phone calls
- 430 women reported indecent suggestions

These figures represent the *number* of women who reported to the survey that they had experienced these incidents at some time in the past. They do not indicate how many incidents were actually experienced. Thus the many instances of multiple victimization were not reflected in the above figures.[5]

Respondents were asked about fear of crime at home and about other situations where they felt 'most at risk': 374 felt most at risk at home. (But as respondents could name more than one situation where they felt most at risk, it is difficult to attach too much significance to this finding.) Three-quarters of respondents reported that they never open the door of their home unless they know who is there. Not surprisingly, 84 per cent of women felt most at risk when walking home alone at night. It was also found that 25 per cent of respondents were afraid to travel in taxis alone at night, and just under a third felt at risk when travelling alone on public transport.

The survey looked in detail at women's experience of rape and sexual assault. As the early BCS research produced relatively little information on these offences, it is worth considering the findings of the Manchester survey. Of the 152 women who reported that they had, at some time, been a victim of rape, over half (57 per cent) knew their attacker. Just under half (47 per cent) of the 266 victims of sexual assault knew the offender. The survey found that 73 per cent of rape victims did not report the incident to the police. The report on the survey expressed concern at this low rate of reporting, stating that something is 'terribly wrong if so many women, having experienced such a horrific crime, [feel that] they cannot report that crime to the police'.[6] The most common reason for non-reporting by rape victims (given by 61 per cent) was that they 'couldn't stand the thought of all their [i.e. the police's] questions'. Respondents were invited to give more than one reason: 39 per cent thought that they would not be believed; 36 per cent thought that the police would not do anything, whilst 30 per cent thought that the police could not do anything; 35 per cent thought the police would be unsympathetic. In relation to sexual assault, 72 per cent of victims did not report the incident to the police. The report summarized these responses as follows:

> It seems that women don't expect the police to believe them, certainly in the cases where the assailant is known to them or if they are out late or there are reasons why they feel the police will blame them. Even if there is strong evidence of the offence women tend to feel that they will be blamed, or even if the police do believe them and don't blame them there is little chance of the rapist being brought to justice and therefore reporting him will only leave them open to possible retaliation.[7]

Of those rape victims who did report the incident to the police, only one indicated that this led to the offender being apprehended. In the case of sexual assault, six out of the seventy-one who reported incidents said that their attacker was caught. Many of those who reported rape or sexual assault revealed their dissatisfaction with the police response. Some felt that the police implied it was their own fault, and in some cases there was a lack of understanding and sympathy for the victim. Others complained of a lack of privacy, lengthy questioning, lack of toilet facilities, lack of information and hostile or flippant attitudes of officers.

In summary, the Manchester survey generated some interesting information despite its methodological shortcomings. The actual numbers of victims are of only limited value, for reasons considered earlier, but the impressions and experiences of victims are still of considerable value. In focusing on women victims and crimes of violence, the survey was able to provide more information on a relatively neglected area. Problems of embarrassment and lack of privacy, which can inhibit a candid response to interviewers in other surveys, did not arise due to the use of a questionnaire which was simply to be completed and returned (free of charge).

Researchers have always experienced difficulties in attempting to quantify sexual assaults. It was also observed, by Chambers and Millar,[8] that researchers had not investigated how victims of these crimes feel about the police or about reporting an incident. Although the Manchester survey did not overcome all the methodological problems inherent in studying this type of victimization, it should not be dismissed out of hand. When one considers how little information on sexual assault was generated by the initial sweep of the BCS, the Manchester survey and other studies are of interest even if they are not directly comparable (because of totally different survey periods and methodologies). Other research on this topic may also briefly be noted, such as Stanko's study in Leeds, in which she interviewed a sample of 129 women. Out of this sample, she found that three respondents had suffered rape and one had been the victim of an attempted rape. She also found that around two-thirds of the sample had experienced some sort of violence.[9] The incidence of sexual assault has also been considered in other regional surveys, some of which are considered below. Interestingly, the Islington Crime Survey found the assumption that female respondents will not reveal such incidents to male interviewers to be erroneous.

The Newham Crime Survey (1986)

A more detailed and sophisticated local survey was carried out on behalf of the London Borough of Newham, in 1986, using professional interviewers from the Harris Research Centre.[10] Although designated an 'Outer London Borough', Newham's rate of recorded crime is comparable to inner-city areas and the crime survey was designed to study both the incidence of crime and the consequences of that crime for those living in the area. A further social problem in the area is the frequency of racially motivated harassment of ethnic minority residents. This was studied in the survey by means of an ethnic minority booster sample and a separate questionnaire on the subject of harassment for all ethnic minority respondents.

The survey was conducted by interviewing a random sample of 784 residents (the 'main sample') throughout the Borough of Newham, using a general or 'screening' questionnaire. Details of incidents, where relevant, were recorded on the victim forms, together with questions about the impact of the offence upon the victim. As the main sample did not provide a sufficient number of Asian and Afro-Caribbean respondents on which to base the study of racial harassment, a booster sample was taken, so as to produce a combined total of 262 Asian and 211 Afro-Caribbean respondents in the overall sample. A separate 'harassment questionnaire' was answered by all Asian and Afro-Caribbean respondents. Sampling and selection of respondents at each address were carried out in a rigorous manner. The 784 residents interviewed represented a comparatively low response rate of 59 per cent of all possible contacts. When the results from both the random and booster samples were combined, the resulting figures were weighted to compensate for the overrepresentation of young ethnic minority respondents in the sample. (It should be noted that *all* respondents answered the general questionnaire, whilst ethnic minority respondents answered the harassment questionnaire in addition to the general one. All victims, from both samples, were interviewed using the victim forms.) Overall, the methodology comprised some elements of the BCS and also had common elements with other local studies, such as the Islington Crime Survey (see below). A novel feature of the Newham project was its inclusion of a racial harassment survey. The findings of both the general and the racial harassment surveys will be considered.

As with other local surveys, such as Merseyside, respondents were asked about the social problems in their area before progressing to more specific questions about crime. Together with unemployment, crime was identified by respondents as one of the largest social problems in their area: 71 per cent of the sample thought that crime was a problem. Many different groups (such as Asians, white women, those aged under twenty-five, those aged over sixty, and home owners) felt that crime was the biggest social problem in their area. Respondents were also asked about the causes of crime in their area: 80 per cent thought that unemployment was a possible cause and 76 per cent thought that crime occurred because of an insufficiency of other activities for young people in their area. It was felt by 67 per cent of respondents that having too few police officers on the streets was also to blame for the level of crime, and 60 per cent blamed lenient sentences given by local magistrates. Inefficient and unresponsive policing was also cited as a cause of crime by many respondents.

Residents were also asked which offences should be given the greatest priority by the police in their area. Burglary was identified as the most important (by 44 per cent), with personal assault (37 per cent) and vandalism or criminal damage (34 per cent) the next largest priorities identified by respondents. Ethnic minority respondents were particularly concerned about racially motivated attacks, and women, in general, thought that the police should pay greater attention to crimes against the person as opposed to property offences.

In relation to fear of crime, 30 per cent of respondents were worried 'a great deal' about being a victim of crime, whilst 23 per cent felt a 'fair amount' of worry; 24 per cent were not worried very much, and 22 per cent were 'not at all' worried. Female respondents were more likely than the men to be worried about crime (65 per cent of women were very or fairly worried, compared with 41 per cent of men). Asian respondents reported particularly high levels of worry about being a victim of crime. Of all Asian respondents, 64 per cent were very or fairly worried, as were 69 per cent of Asians aged over forty-five, and 75 per cent of Asian women. The particular offences which caused the greatest levels of worry for respondents were – in descending order – burglary, vandalism to the home and other property, street robbery, car theft, assault and being insulted and threatened. Worry about sexual assault was very common (68 per cent) amongst female respondents, and women were generally more fearful about all types of crime except car theft.

To what extent did fear of crime affect the behaviour of residents? Just over half of the total sample were worried (either very or fairly) about being out of their homes after dark, in contrast to 69 per cent of Asian respondents and 86 per cent of Asian women. Women were much more worried than men about going out after dark (i.e. 72 per cent as opposed to 33 per cent of the men). In relation to feeling safe in their own homes, Asian respondents were once again more worried than other residents. Whilst 60 per cent of the total sample never felt unsafe at home, only 45 per cent of Asian respondents felt similarly secure. Interestingly, female respondents in general felt much less safe at home than the men who were interviewed: only 52 per cent of women never felt unsafe in their own home.

The survey found that 22 per cent of respondents had been a victim, at least once, of a crime covered by the survey during the previous twelve months. (This figure excludes the racial harassment incidents which were dealt with separately.) Asian residents had a slightly higher victimization rate (25 per cent) than white residents (20 per cent), but not significantly so. Men were more frequently victimized than women, and social classes ABC1 were also more at risk than other groups. This is an interesting finding, as it is at odds with other victimization research which suggests that it is the less well-off sections of society who more frequently experience victimization. Of course, there may well be differential rates of reporting to the survey, as respondents from certain social groups may be more willing to identify an incident as criminal or, indeed, be more adept at answering the survey questions. Older residents were least at risk of victimization, and the highest rate of victimization was experienced by the 25–44 age group, with slightly lower levels recorded by the 16–24 age group.

Burglary was the most common crime, suffered by 6 per cent of respondents, followed by theft from a vehicle (5 per cent), attempted burglary (4 per cent), vandalism (4 per cent), theft from the person (3 per cent), personal assault (2 per cent), threat of assault (2 per cent), violent street robbery (2 per cent), theft of motor vehicle (2 per cent), and theft from the home (2 per cent). The survey found that half of all victims suffered two or more crimes during the past twelve months. Thus, once again, the phenomenon of repeat or multiple victimization was illustrated by these findings.

The main survey revealed 522 crimes experienced by respondents, of which 299 were reported to the police. This reporting rate (of 57 per cent) is quite high, although it naturally varied considerably from one offence category to another. Whilst over three-quarters of all burglaries were reported, under a quarter of threats of assault were brought to the attention of the police. Over half of all respondents felt that the police had a good understanding of local problems, but ethnic minority respondents had a less favourable view of the adequacy of police understanding. Looking at all respondents, 9 per cent thought that the police were very effective in dealing with local crime, 37 per cent thought they were fairly effective, 25 per cent said 'not very effective', and 11 per cent 'not at all effective'. Once again, levels of dissatisfaction with police performance were much higher amongst ethnic minority residents. For example, for Asian respondents, the percentages were: 3 per cent (very effective), 26 per cent (fairly effective), 26 per cent (not very effective), 26 per cent (not at all effective), with 19 per cent undecided. Similarly, Asian respondents gave a less favourable assessment of the police response to incidents which they had reported.

The public also come into contact with the police, albeit less often, in circumstances which are initiated by the police.[11] The most common reason for this type of contact is in relation to a road traffic incident or offence. The Newham report suggested a good deal of dissatisfaction and resentment, especially amongst Afro-Caribbean and Asian respondents. Whereas 53 per cent of white respondents felt that they were treated fairly by the police during such incidents, only 21 per cent of Afro-Caribbeans and 34 per cent of Asians felt that their treatment was fair.

The Newham survey studied police–public contact in considerable depth and not all of its findings will be dealt with here. But it is worth noting the shift in emphasis which took place in many local surveys, such as that of Newham, with the victimization study being used as a means to try to make police performance and priorities more accountable to the local population. For this reason, the public were asked about policing priorities and the responsiveness of the police to a wide range of issues. There are obviously limitations on the use of the resulting findings, but this aspect of the research is a good example of the more political orientation of victimization research. A problem with such evidence (for example, on the number of residents dissatisfied with the police response to various types of incident) is that the police may be made a focal point for all types of dissatisfaction and may be blamed for the shortcomings of other institutions, such as the courts or other areas of local administration.

A further problem with certain questions which were included about the police is that respondents were simply not able to give informed opinions, and therefore it is difficult to see the point of their inclusion. For example, respondents were asked whether the police ought to use stop-and-search powers more or less often. But, as the survey found, many respondents were simply unable to answer such a question as they had no direct experience of this practice. Even more redundant was the question which asked whether the police use undue pressure when interviewing people. As only around 1 per cent of the sample had actually been arrested and taken to the police station within the survey period, it is not surprising that a large number (38 per cent) did not feel able to judge whether the police were over zealous when interrogating suspects. But it must be questioned how useful are the views of the 62 per cent of respondents who did have some opinion about police behaviour in interviews. People are being asked about matters of which they have little direct experience or knowledge. This is inviting either an ill-informed response, or, perhaps worse, the respondent is being invited to offer received opinions on the subject. So if respondents have heard of criticisms of the police (in relation to the use of stop-and-search powers), they might feel that this is the opportunity to express a politically correct opinion. They may even feel that such a response is expected by the interviewer.

These criticisms may seem pedantic or harsh, but they do touch upon an important issue. Victimization surveys are very useful for recording certain types of factual information, even allowing for much subjective interpretation and human error and, up to a point, they can provide some indication of opinions about and responses to crime. But it is possible to push the methodology too far in using surveys as a means of monitoring and evaluating various aspects of police practice which, for the most part, are beyond the scope of respondents' personal experience and knowledge. For these reasons, the findings on certain aspects of police practice are to be treated with caution.

The section on respondents' evaluation of police performance and conduct was concluded by asking whether they were pleased with their treatment by the police during the last five years. Even allowing for the fact that many respondents had not had any direct contact with the police during this period, those that had experienced some contact were more likely to be displeased rather than pleased with their treatment. For all respondents, 24 per cent were pleased, 41 per cent were not pleased and 35 per cent had no contact. For Afro-Caribbean respondents, 14 per cent were pleased, 58 per cent were not pleased and 28 per cent had no contact. A mere 16 per cent of Asian respondents were pleased with their treatment by the police, as opposed to 49 per cent who were displeased (with 33 per cent experiencing no contact during the relevant period). The only group of respondents which described themselves as more pleased than displeased, was the 45–59 age group of white respondents. Victims of crime and racial harassment were particularly unhappy about their treatment. The report stated:

> One in five residents reported that they had been annoyed by the police in some way in the past five years. This figure reached higher levels among Afro-Caribbean residents . . . when contact takes place between the police and the public very few members of the public come away happy with the treatment they received.[12]

It is not to deny that there may well be high levels of dissatisfaction amongst local residents about their contacts with the police in Newham (and many other areas). But, again, it might be questioned whether the findings of the survey on this issue can be regarded as clear evidence of such dissatisfaction. The number of reasons given by respondents for their displeasure were very wide-ranging and included quite a large number who complained that the police had done little to help when an incident had been reported to them. Therefore, the annoyance experienced by many respondents might equally have been described as frustration at the lack of progress made in dealing with their incident. However, it must be emphasized that many of the reasons given for displeasure did reveal well-founded grievances and certainly support the case for a more responsive and sensitive policing of that area.

An important feature of the Newham survey was the inclusion of questions on racial harassment. The report stated that only one in twenty of such incidents were reported, and the writers attributed this mainly to a lack of confidence in the police (although non-reporting of other offences has been shown in most surveys to be associated with the trivial nature of the incident and a feeling that the police would be unable to do anything about it).[13] The racial harassment questionnaire dealt with respondents' attitudes to a variety of social problems facing ethnic minority residents in Newham, as well as concentrating on racial harassment incidents during the twelve-month period covered by the survey.

The survey found that a quarter of ethnic minority residents had been victims of some form of racial harassment. This term covered a variety of incidents such as insulting behaviour, damage to property, assault and theft. Asian respondents reported a higher rate of victimization (28 per cent) than Afro-Caribbeans (22 per cent). Unlike victimization rates for other crimes, harassment was experienced quite evenly throughout the different age groups. Racial assaults occurred three times more often than general assaults recorded in the main survey. In total, the 116 victims of harassment between them disclosed 1,550 incidents during the survey period, of which around half (774) were incidents of insulting behaviour. There were 175 incidents of attempted theft, 188 incidents of attempted damage to property, 174 cases of threatened damage or violence, 153 cases of physical assault, and 40 incidents of actual criminal damage or vandalism. As we have seen, the rate of reporting of incidents to the police was very low (around 5 per cent). Even in relation to the incidents which were felt by respondents to be the most important ones, only a third were reported to the police.

Where incidents were reported, there was a disturbingly high rate of dissatisfaction with the police's handling of the matter, with 52 per cent feeling very dissatisfied and 29 per cent fairly dissatisfied. Whilst some respondents felt dissatisfaction because the police were unable to take any effective action, others were annoyed because the police did not appear to show any, or sufficient, interest in their incident. (In fact, in only 1 per cent of incidents did respondents feel that their case was given a high priority by the police.) A mere 18 per cent of harassment victims received any advice or support from any organization. In addition to widespread dissatisfaction with police performance in response to racial harassment incidents, there was also disquiet about the perceived inaction of the local council. Around 60 per cent of ethnic minority respondents felt that the Newham Council ought to be more actively involved in tackling this problem, although many respondents were not sure how this could be practically achieved, except by exerting greater influence over the police to improve their performance.

When asked for suggestions on tackling harassment, many of the responses involved some suggestions about policing; for example, more visible policing, better training and greater willingness to take action. Part of the problem is that the police were also identified as the source of a good deal of the harassment suffered by ethnic minority residents.[14] For example, around one half of Afro-Caribbean respondents were of the opinion that police harassment was a problem in Newham, and this view was shared by an even larger proportion of young Afro-Caribbean residents. The report on this section of the survey concluded:

> The seriousness of the problem of racial harassment in Newham is beyond question. The basic problem is further compounded by a strongly held view amongst black residents that the police are doing little to tackle the problem. The degree of distrust with which the police are viewed by black residents is profound and it is clear that it is related to the view that the police are doing little to aid the black community.[15]

In summary, the Newham survey, whilst loosely based on the British Crime Survey methodology, showed a very different orientation and purpose to the national study. It was less scientific and more political with its use of findings to make prescriptive comments. It included a very useful section on racial harassment which was, at the time, fairly innovative. But it also shows clearly the tendency to use surveys to gather attitudes and opinions on matters which are not always within the respondents' sphere of competence to answer. There are dangers in reading too much into respondents' attitudes which are not based on relevant personal experience. There *is* a valid case for campaigning for greater police accountability to the local community, but it is far from clear that victimization surveys are the best means of advancing this cause.[16]

The Merseyside Crime Survey 1984

This research, directed by Richard Kinsey, was commissioned by the Merseyside Metropolitan Council in 1984. Out of a total population of one and a half million, a sample of 3,500 people were interviewed in the Merseyside area, in what was one of the first large-scale regional surveys of its type.[17] This survey, together with the Islington Crime Survey (discussed below), has been described as representing the 'new realist' wave of surveys,[18] so characterized for its 'new sense of mission' to use victim research to expose social injustice and not simply to gather better information on crime rates. As with the Newham survey, there was a central focus on victims' experiences and attitudes, especially in relation to policing in their area. As it is intended to look in some detail at the Islington survey, to illustrate this trend in victimization research, only brief mention will be made of the Merseyside survey.[19]

The Merseyside survey report emphasized the high risk of victimization for the poor and the socially disadvantaged. It argued that these statistics were more relevant than estimates derived from the British Crime Survey which appeared to play down the risk of victimization for the 'statistically average' person. Once again, the approach was more overtly political. In discussing the Merseyside and other research findings, Kinsey, Lea and Young stated:

> Mrs Thatcher tells us that crime is unrelated to unemployment and poverty. She shuts her eyes to the economic apartheid which now divides the north from the Home Counties and the outer council estates from affluent Finchley. The insurance companies know better. In inner-city Liverpool in 1986 one home in four will be broken into, and one in ten people will have their homes or persons searched by the police. So the building societies will not lend on their houses, the insurance companies double their premiums, and on top of that local government spending is strangled by Westminster.[20]

In the inner-city areas covered by the Merseyside survey, crime was regarded as second only to unemployment as the largest social problem. Anxiety about crime was found to be realistic amongst the socially and economically vulnerable: those who were most worried were also found to have the highest risk of victimization and multiple victimization. It was the poor who experienced the highest rates of crime and also suffered most as a consequence of incidents. This was a widespread problem, as there were 300,000 Merseyside residents living in some of the worst council accommodation in Britain. Working-class women, in particular, were found to be the most severely affected group. In contrast to some previous surveys, the Merseyside research uncovered high rates of victimization amongst female respondents, especially when sexual and other harassment incidents were included in the statistics. The survey also found that 20 per cent of all respondents did not go out after dark because of fear of crime and, in inner-city areas, fear of crime had an even greater impact on residents' lifestyles.

In addition to the 3,500 Merseyside residents interviewed for the crime survey between May and July 1984, a second survey of 1,190 Merseyside police officers was also carried out by the same researchers in October to December 1984. Together, the two surveys form a major investigation of crime, victimization and policing in the region. The crime survey found, as with many other studies, that a large proportion of respondents (79 per cent) wanted to see more police officers on the beat (that is, on foot patrol), which they felt would represent a deterrent to crime by their presence. (Indeed, 90 per cent of North Birkenhead residents wished to see a greater number of foot patrol police officers in their area.) The three main priorities which Merseyside respondents wanted the police to pursue were: to provide an immediate response to emergencies, which was identified by 90 per cent as a 'very important police task'; to investigate crime (80 per cent); and to provide a deterrent 'street' presence (74 per cent). To what extent did the performance of the police measure up to these expectations? A useful feature of conducting a second survey, to look at, *inter alia*, police organization and the use of police time, was that this question could be fully explored.

The Survey of Merseyside Police Officers (hereafter the MPO survey) found that foot patrol work was heavily associated with young and inexperienced officers. Virtually half of Merseyside foot patrol officers were under twenty-five years of age, many of whom were relatively new to the job.[21] Thus, it could be questioned whether the priority which the public wanted to be given to patrol work was, in fact, being given by the police, in view of the deployment of so many young and inexperienced officers on this type of work. A further problem was that this type of police work was not particularly popular with officers, who were generally interested in more specialist areas, such as CID or traffic. It would seem that patrol work lacks status amongst police officers. Kinsey summed up some of the problems of police organization and deployment as follows:

> Both the youthfulness of regular patrol officers and the disproportionately low number of women in different ways may contribute to the distancing of the police from certain sections of the community. Claims that the police are distanced from the communities within which they work are not without foundation. Across the force, 81% of police officers live outside the divisions in which they work, 57% said they had neither close friends nor relatives in the area and 47% said they spent none of their leisure time in the division. There is reason to believe from the Merseyside Crime Survey that in some areas – especially in those where crime rates are high – informal contact between police and public will be minimal.[22]

The MPO survey also studied how the various officers spent their working days. This enabled the researchers to look at how much of a patrol officer's time was left free for simply keeping 'an eye open' and was not strictly directed towards a specific task. It was found that, for the force as a whole, only 44 per cent of police time was spent actually outside police premises. Overall, around 25 per cent of police time was occupied by administration and paperwork, whilst only 16 per cent of time was occupied by non-directed patrol work. Furthermore, just 6 per cent of police time was spent on interviewing informants, witnesses or suspects.[23]

Providing an immediate response to emergency calls was seen as a very important police task by 90 per cent of Merseyside Crime Survey respondents, and 80 per cent thought that the investigation of crime was very important. The MPO survey found that responding to emergency calls from the public did not take up a great deal of police time. Around 10 per cent of mobile patrol officers' time was spent on this, and only 3 per cent of police time as a whole was occupied by this function. Also, as we have seen, just 6 per cent of police time was devoted to interviewing suspects, informants and witnesses, despite the central importance of this activity to catching offenders.[24] The Merseyside Crime Survey also found that around 25 per cent of victims who reported the incident to the police voiced some dissatisfaction with the police response. The reasons for this dissatisfaction were most likely to be either police lack of action or failure to help. So it would seem that the police could enhance their performance and their standing in the eyes of the public, if they were to attach greater importance to responding more energetically to reports of incidents from the public, and especially from victims.

It seems that, in general terms, the Merseyside officers shared the public's view that more foot patrol officers were needed. But the irony was that the majority of officers did not want such a job for themselves. The reality of such work, with its low status and exposure to the elements, was not glamorous in the eyes of those who were doing it or those who had recently experienced it. The MPO survey found that morale amongst foot patrol officers was fairly low; it was certainly lower than in the force as a whole. This was thought to reflect a sense of isolation from colleagues and senior officers.

The Islington Crime Survey 1985

The Islington Crime Survey (ICS) is another good example of a major regional survey with a new realist orientation. It is proposed to concentrate on the first survey of 1985, although it should be noted that a second survey was carried out in 1988. (Accordingly, references to the ICS or 'the survey' which follow, apply to the 1985 survey unless it is specifically stated otherwise.) The ICS was conducted by researchers from the Middlesex Polytechnic (as it then was) Centre for Criminology in 1985. In the introduction to their report on the survey, the authors made direct reference to the potential contribution of victimization surveys to a programme of social reform and social justice.[25] It was observed that as crime and its effects are not experienced equally throughout society, to talk in terms of 'statistically average' risks of victimization is unhelpful. The authors wished to focus their concern on those sections of society which experience victimization most frequently. Jones et al. stated: 'If you add to the concern for blacks as victims a concern for the working class, for the poor, for the vulnerable and for women, you have an understanding of the realist approach to crime today.'[26]

It was pointed out that despite the usefulness of the British Crime Survey programme, this research was not able 'to deal with the fundamental fact that crime is both geographically and socially focused'.[27] This is why regional surveys are required to build on the pioneering work done by the Home Office researchers in the national survey. But, as noted earlier, the emphasis in the regional surveys (like those of Merseyside and Islington) moved away from just 'mapping' crime and victimization, to looking more directly at police–public relations and police performance in relation to crime – as perceived by victims and the public at large. In addition to inquiring about well-established offences, the ICS also included questions about more general types of harassment, interracial incidents and drug use.

The ICS was commissioned by the Islington Borough Council and it involved an in-depth study of crime and policing in a (generally) poor inner-city area, with high unemployment and severe housing problems. The researchers took both a general sample of people over sixteen years old in Islington, and also an ethnic minority booster sample. They aimed at an overall sample size of 2,000, of whom 400 were to be allocated to the booster sample.[28] Crime was regarded by respondents in Islington as the most serious social problem after unemployment. Indeed, by the time of the second survey in that area, in 1988, crime was identified as the most serious problem.[29] Levels of fear of crime were also high, particularly in relation to burglary, robbery, rape and vandalism. The researchers did not agree with the view that residents' perceptions of crime were a reflection of media distortion. They felt that respondents' perception of risk was frequently an accurate assessment of their potential vulnerability.

The ICS found that the crime rate in Islington, where comparison was possible, was much higher than the national rate of offending as calculated by the British Crime Survey. It was also found that, in general, the reporting rate of incidents in Islington was higher than the national average. On the other hand, the researchers found that the proportion of reported incidents which were recorded by the police was smaller than the national average, leading them to conclude that

although the rates of crime are higher, the reporting rates to the police are higher and the percentage of actual crimes committed recorded in the police statistics are higher, the police recording of reported offences is less than the national average.[30]

The researchers questioned whether Islington residents were getting as good a service from their police officers as the rest of the country. They found that a further problem was the unwillingness of the police to co-operate with certain sections of the population as readily as the police do in other parts of the country, with the result that some groups were effectively alienated from the police. The ICS also asked victims their reasons for not reporting incidents (where applicable) and found that the most common reason given was that the victim thought that it would achieve nothing. Once again, this tends to suggest that many victims lack confidence in their local police in Islington.

The Islington researchers found a good deal of agreement amongst the public as to which offences should be given priority by the police. Respondents thought that robbery with violence in the street, assaults on women, use of hard drugs, burglary, drunken driving, and racist attacks, should be treated as the priority offences by the police (in that order). There was also widespread agreement as to what should be regarded as the least important offences, at least in terms of occupying police time and resources. These were prostitution, use of cannabis, unruly behaviour in the street, shoplifting and company fraud. The researchers found that it was not true to say that certain groups or 'subcultures' had very different priorities from the rest of the local population. Taking the example of young Afro-Caribbean residents, it was shown that their view of the offences which should most occupy police time was virtually the same as the rest of the sample – with the exception that racist attacks were placed as first priority on their list. As the authors of the report on the ICS observed, this hardly suggests a subculture which has widely different values, or views, on policing from the rest of society.[31]

The researchers asked respondents to assess the effectiveness of the police in dealing with a range of offences (seven in all). In relation to offences which the public regarded as high-priority crimes, such as street robbery, sexual assault and burglary, the majority of respondents (over 50 per cent at least) thought that the police were unsuccessful in dealing with these crimes. It was only in relation to street fighting and unruly teenage behaviour that a majority thought that the police were successful in dealing with offences. Although the researchers state correctly that this is a cause for concern, the conclusion to be drawn from these particular findings should be guarded. It does suggest a lack of confidence in the police, which may or may not be well informed, but it could also be that the police are made the focus of respondents' justifiable grievances about other aspects of the criminal justice system and other social agencies. This is not to deny the potential importance of the ICS findings on public perception of the police; it is merely to suggest some caution in interpreting the data.

ICS respondents were also asked whether the police in their own area dealt with all types of residents in an even-handed manner. A third of respondents thought that some groups were not treated equally or fairly by the police. But this overall figure masks considerable differences of opinion within the sample. For example, of those aged over forty-five, only 13 per cent thought that the police did not treat people fairly and equally, whereas 54 per cent of those aged 16–24 held this opinion. Moreover, whilst only around one third of white and Asian respondents thought the police were not even-handed, nearly two-thirds of Afro-Caribbean respondents were of this opinion. It was also found that those who thought that the police did not react unfairly to certain groups were more likely not to have had contact with the police. The greater the frequency of respondents' contact with the police, the less likely they were to feel that the police deal even-handedly with all groups. Similarly, respondents who have been victims of crime were also less likely to think that the police react fairly to all groups. For example, only 22 per cent of non-victims felt that the police treat some groups unfairly, whereas 35 per cent of those victimized once or twice held this opinion, as did 43 per cent of three times (or more) victims.

Respondents were also asked whether the police had a good understanding of the area's problems, and one third thought that they had not. Once more, it was older respondents who tended to take a favourable view of the police's understanding, with young respondents being the most critical. Also, Afro-Caribbean respondents were more likely to doubt the police's understanding of the area than other groups. The survey also asked respondents for their views on the frequency of police misconduct, specifically in relation to the use of undue force in arresting suspects, using violence at the police station, 'planting' evidence, and accepting bribes. The ICS found that Islington residents were more likely to believe that such malpractices occur than were residents in London as a whole.[32] In Islington, about half of the respondents felt that these types of police misconduct actually occur. Furthermore, 21 per cent of respondents thought that undue force was frequently used to arrest people, and the same percentage thought that evidence was often planted on people. Once again, young people and Afro-Caribbeans were more likely to believe both that the police use undue force, and that they often do so. Of course, it is not possible to know how well informed these opinions of respondents are, but these findings reveal a considerable scepticism about police probity and adherence to the law. The researchers also dismiss the idea that the public's declining faith in police standards, also evidenced by the ICS, can be attributed to the sensationalism or distortion of the press and television. As they rightly pointed out, media influence alone would not account for the more sceptical attitude of Islington respondents when compared with London residents as a whole.

The ICS estimated that 1,190 cases of sexual assault occurred in Islington during the survey period. It was further estimated that around one in five of these incidents was reported to the police and about 9 per cent were recorded in the criminal statistics. (These figures include *all* types of sexual assault, including rapes.) When the different categories of sexual assault were broken down for analysis, it was found that 50 per cent of rapes were reported to the police, whereas the reporting rate for sexual assaults was 13 per cent (where one assailant was involved) and only 6.5 per cent (where there was more than one assailant). It is surprising that both for rape and sexual assault, incidents involving more than one attacker had lower reporting rates by victims than incidents involving a lone offender. It was also estimated that almost a quarter of all sexual assaults were offences of rape or attempted rape. These statistics on sexual assault present a very different picture from the British Crime Survey estimates discussed in the previous chapter. Also, given the greater sophistication of the methodology used by the ICS researchers, these findings are much more reliable than the Manchester survey of women victims and certain other studies which have been conducted on this subject.

The survey found that women aged 16–24 were much more likely to be sexually assaulted than women in the older age groups. Afro-Caribbean women appeared slightly less likely than white women to be victims of sexual assault, but this may have been due to a greater reluctance on their part to disclose incidents to interviewers. Not surprisingly, women who went out frequently in the evenings were more at risk of being sexually assaulted, as were women who were employed and women who rented private accommodation. The researchers suggested that as a woman's economic independence increases, so too does her likelihood of being a victim of sexual assault, except for women in the higher earning group who appeared to be less at risk of victimization.

In addition to crimes of sexual assault and domestic violence, women were found to be more frequently the victims of certain other offences, such as theft from the person. There is a further problem for women in that some of the crimes which are most commonly committed against them are not accorded much priority by the police. For example, in relation to incidents of domestic violence, harassment and assault, many victims complain of unsympathetic police attitudes. (Also see the results of the Manchester survey, discussed at the start of this chapter.) Because of this perception of police lack of sympathy in dealing with reported incidents, this in turn can lead to victims becoming even more reluctant to report offences to them.

The ICS attempted to provide a more searching investigation of women's perceptions and experience of crime, and of issues relating to their safety. For this reason, questions were also included to look at the incidence of non-criminal harassment of women in Islington. The researchers stated:

> Sometimes women have to endure lewd comments in the street, the persistence of kerb crawlers, and unwanted sexual advances, both from strangers and acquaintances. Sometimes women find themselves in frightening and potentially volatile situations, such as being followed by strangers, where the threat of physical harm due to sexual or physical assault is present. Such forms of non-criminal street violence, together with the threat of criminal victimization aimed strictly at women, serve to produce a very different reality for women than for men, and it was felt that this reality probably has an effect on both women's attitudes and their behaviours [*sic*]. Therefore, the survey attempts to measure and analyse both material gender differences and their consequences.[33]

Respondents were asked, *inter alia*, about their perception of risks for women (in general) who go out alone in their area after dark, and also they were asked if they, personally, ever worried about going out on their own after dark. A further question was asked about whether they ever felt unsafe in their own home due to fear of crime. The ICS found that women were much more likely than men to be fearful of going out alone at night. In total, only 27 per cent of male respondents were worried, whereas 72.6 per cent of all female respondents feared for their personal safety outside the home after dark. It is also a cause for concern that more than one third of female respondents felt unsafe at home because of fear of crime.[34] Although it is possible that the fears expressed by many residents, in response to this question, relate to their worries about the safety of other members of their family, particularly their small children.

The ICS also tried to assess how fear of crime affected residents' behaviour. The researchers found that almost 37 per cent of female respondents always avoided going out after dark, in contrast to only 7 per cent of male respondents who adopted such an extreme precaution. Similarly, whilst 23.3 per cent of women tried to lessen their risk of victimization by not going out unaccompanied, a mere 4 per cent of men adopted this risk-avoidance behaviour. (The survey also found that older respondents were more likely to take risk-avoidance precautions.) But women do not necessarily avoid acts of violence by staying at home; a large number of offences committed against women occur at home and are inflicted upon them by people they know well. It should also be noted that assaults on women which were revealed to the ICS suggested that a considerable *level* of violence was frequently inflicted on victims and that this was particularly so in relation to domestic incidents. Taking domestic violence victims as a separate category, the researchers found that 96 per cent received bruises, 45 per cent received cuts, and almost one in ten victims suffered broken bones. It was also found that in around 12 per cent of domestic violence cases an overnight stay in hospital for the victim was necessitated.

As observed earlier, the ICS also investigated the frequency of other types of harassment of respondents which, although falling short of any clearly defined criminal conduct, was nonetheless threatening or intimidating to victims. It was found that women were much more frequently victimized by this type of 'non-criminal street violence' (as it was described) than men. Although such harassment was not a significant problem for older women, it was a fairly frequent experience of younger women, particularly in the 16–24 age group. For example, 30 per cent of female respondents aged 16–24 stated that they had been followed; nearly a quarter had been shouted at or called after, and 21.3 per cent had been pestered by kerb crawlers. (For women in the 25–44 age group, rates of victimization were about half those of the younger group.) Obviously, the types of incident covered by this sort of offensive conduct may vary considerably in seriousness and impact upon the victim. But, despite the fact that a number of comparatively trivial incidents will have been incorporated into these figures, this should not disguise the importance of the researchers' findings. As Jones et al. observed: 'it is precisely these kinds of frightening, threatening or annoying situations which further contribute to the curfew on women.'[35]

The problem for women is exacerbated by the fact that they receive insufficient support from the police and other agencies when they are the victims of violence. Respondents were asked about their satisfaction with the police response to their reported incident. It was found that one third of those who reported domestic violence were not satisfied with the police response. But, even more disturbingly, there was a profound level of dissatisfaction amongst victims of rape and sexual assault who reported their incidents to the police. Indeed, none of the rape victims who reported to the police appeared to be satisfied by the police response, and most victims were highly dissatisfied.[36]

The ICS also attempted to assess the impact of crime on victims. The researchers found, most conclusively, that respondents with the lowest incomes were the ones who generally suffered the most economic loss as a result of their victimization. Poorer people were less likely to be able to afford insurance for their property, or to be able to replace uninsured goods. In summary, they stated that 'after all material factors have been taken into consideration, it is the lower income groups that are hit the hardest by crime.'[37]

The ICS is, therefore, a good example of the new realist development within victimization research. It provided a sharp contrast with early British Crime Survey research, which tended to suggest that a good deal of fear of crime was not necessarily based on actual likelihood of victimization and also failed to highlight the vulnerability of particular groups of people, notably women and ethnic minorities. The ICS focused considerable attention on gender and race as variables in relation to rates of victimization and its effects. The survey discovered high rates of victimization and repeat victimization in the area. For example, although there were an estimated 123 burglaries per 1,000 households, only 9 per cent of households were victimized. This suggests that of those households that were affected, a quarter were repeat victims. Repeat victimization was particularly common in relation to vandalism and assault. It was also found that women experienced victimization more frequently than men, especially in relation to theft from the person and assault, and that, in general, ethnic minorities faced a higher risk of victimization than white residents. The researchers concluded that, far from being unrealistic or exaggerated, respondents' attitudes to crime were broadly consistent with their direct experiences and the actual risks that they faced. In keeping with the use of victimization research to promote social reform and social justice, the ICS also looked in much detail at the interaction between the public and the police, and the public's view of the priorities that the police should pursue.

It is possible to criticize these new realist surveys for reading too much into subjective experiences and attitudes of respondents and losing sight of the limitations of the crime survey methodology. Some critics have suggested that, in an attempt to combat inequality, injustice and unaccountable and unresponsive policing, they may have drawn rather firmer conclusions from their data than was strictly warranted.[38] Whether these criticisms are well founded is open to debate, but it is certainly true to state (as the authors of the ICS acknowledged at the outset) that their mission was not simply to describe or map out crime in that area, but also to attempt to provide explanations and recommendations. Jones et al. concluded their introduction to the ICS report by stating:

> The local survey fits into the upsurge in demand for the democratization of public institutions and the need to fit policy to public demand, particularly in the context of a decentralization of power. As such, the lessons to be learnt from such surveys both about crime and policing have a purchase outside of

the context of a particular inner-city London Borough. They are essential in formulating and implementing policy in this vital area and the results can be applied to the urban heartlands of all Western industrial societies.[39]

Thus victimization surveys, detailing respondents' experiences of and fears about crime, became accepted into the fold of the radical criminology perspective. This was particularly evident when it was realized that such surveys could go beyond merely studying victims, to assessing the role of the police and public attitudes to policing and a variety of social problems. Not surprisingly, it was areas that were perceived as having a high crime rate that were the focus of most attention from local councils and researchers: hence the studies in Nottingham, Islington, Newham, Merseyside and Manchester. But if we are concerned with qualitative, as well as quantitative information, people's experience of and anxieties about crime in more sparsely populated areas are of no less interest. What progress has been made with this type of research?

Surveying Crime in Rural Areas

In the past, the vast majority of studies of crime and victimology have concentrated on densely populated areas. Put simply, crime is often regarded as a largely urban problem. Yet it will be remembered from the opening chapter that recent statistical analyses have suggested that some of the traditionally high-crime areas have been overtaken by areas which were formerly thought to be less crime-ridden. For example, in the recent House of Commons computer analysis of crime statistics, it was suggested that households in Gloucestershire and Avon had a higher risk of being burgled than those in the Merseyside area. (The difficulties of interpreting such figures have been looked at earlier and it is not intended to evaluate this research here.) There is growing interest today in investigating issues of crime, victimization and policing strategies in less densely populated areas.[40]

We can take a recent example, which relates to the experience of racial minorities in rural areas. Although racial harassment is correctly perceived as a serious problem in many urban areas, the prevalence of this type of behaviour is not so well documented in other parts of the country. Recently, however, the Norwich and Norfolk Racial Equality Council conducted a small survey, interviewing seventy people from racial minority groups and also sending questionnaires to around 150 local organizations. It was estimated that ethnic minorities represented approximately 1 per cent of the local population in the area; yet members of these groups frequently suffered harassment and hostility on the housing estates on which they live, and were often subjected to offensive remarks at work.[41] The report stated:

> Racism is a problem associated in the popular imagination with inner cities. The media stereotype tells that black people are concentrated in poor quality jobs and in poor quality housing, threatening the traditional way of life and livelihood of the white indigenous population. In Norfolk this does not exist. Those black or Asian people that white people do meet are encountered individually and therefore constitute no real threat.[42]

In view of disturbing findings such as these, we should be cautious in accepting some of the traditionally held views about crime and related problems in rural areas. In any case, crime rates alone tell us very little about local communities' experience of crime, their levels of fear and their relationship with the local police. We may wish to inquire why some areas have a relatively low rate of recorded crime, and to see what lessons can be learnt from these low-crime areas. To what extent do some areas rely more heavily on informal methods of social control to prevent or reduce crime? These are questions which can usefully be pursued by researchers. An interesting study of the experience of crime and policing in a rural community, together with a comparison of crime in an urban area, was carried out by Joanna Shapland and Jon Vagg.[43] Although this research used observational methods and semi-structured interviews with residents, and was not a victimization survey in the sense in which this term has been used so far, it is intended to include its findings here because of the paucity of research on rural areas in general.

Shapland and Vagg studied two groups of villages in the Midlands. One was a large village of nearly 2,000 residents, which they called 'Southton'. The other village – it was in fact a group of villages – had a similar, but slightly smaller population, and the researchers referred to it as 'Northam'. It was pointed out that despite being rural areas, many of the houses in these villages were located very close together and, therefore, that the population densities were comparable to some of the urban districts which the researchers looked at in the second part of their study. A considerable amount of the housing in the two villages was of the small terraced type, with adjoining walls, and much of the parking was 'on-street', rather than in private garages. In short, the physical location of residents was not significantly less conducive (at least potentially) to noisy disturbances and vandalism to vehicles and property than in the urban areas. In addition to these villages, the researchers also studied four small urban areas in a Midlands city. They did not find such pronounced disparities in residents' perceptions of their respective areas as one might have originally expected. Shapland and Vagg stated:

> The people we interviewed tried to convey to us what they felt to be distinctively communal about their own neighbourhood. In fact, we found the difference between rural and urban areas to be matters of degree, rather than marks of a rural/urban divide. There was considerable similarity between the social processes in the rural and urban areas . . . [F]or some factors, such as the extent of social networks, Southton seemed more similar to the urban area than to Northam.[44]

The researchers looked at the official crime statistics for the area covered by their study. The two adjacent police 'beats', in which all four of the urban areas were included, were situated close to the city centre and contained many commercial as well as residential premises. Although both of these urban police areas had crime rates which were above the national average, one had a significantly higher crime rate than the other. The crime rates in the areas which included the villages were conspicuously below the national rate. (It should be remembered that the relative absence of commercial premises from the village areas would have been at least partly responsible for this.) It should also be emphasized that these figures represent the level of recorded crimes in each of the relevant areas. The low official crime rates in the villages might have been a reflection of low reporting rates by victims. The types of crimes committed in the villages were basically similar to those in the urban areas; it was simply that they occurred much less frequently. One interesting difference, however, was that in the rural areas, the property crimes were committed against private individuals in only about 50 per cent of incidents (the rest being committed against shops, pubs, companies, the council etc.); whereas in the urban areas, a large majority of property offences were directed against private individuals. This is slightly surprising and perhaps the opposite of what one might have expected. It could be that commercial premises in urban areas have better protection against theft, burglary and vandalism.

The survey also studied the public's use of police services by looking, *inter alia*, at the messages received and recorded by the police in both the rural and urban areas. In relation to the size of the population, the police received far more calls in the urban areas: that is, over 9,000 calls per 100,000 population in the towns, compared to around 2,700 calls per 100,000 in the villages. The researchers found that, despite their lesser frequency, calls from the public in the rural areas followed a broadly similar pattern to those of the urban areas in terms of their subject matter. Moreover, Shapland and Vagg did not find it particularly helpful to categorize calls as either crime-related or service-oriented. They rightly pointed out that many calls did not fit neatly under one of these headings as opposed to the other and, therefore, that attempts to measure the public's demand on police services by means of this dichotomy were unreliable. They observed:

> Categorization becomes, moreover, almost immaterial when one considers that 'crime' is itself a social construction, built up in discussions and negotiations between police officers and members of the public involved as victims, witnesses, and offenders. The usefulness of employing the notion of 'crime' . . . is apparent to all parties in the case of property crime which has obviously occurred. 'Crime' may not be at all a useful or pertinent idea in the case of minor assaults, rowdiness, disturbances created by mentally disturbed persons, and the like, when both public and police really want the immediate problem to calm down or stop and the cause of the disturbance to go away . . .[45]

The researchers found that the public's reports of property offences were usually well founded and, for the most part, were acted upon by the police. In relation to reports of disturbances, official action was taken much less frequently by the police. (In the rural areas, for example, in just 9 per cent of such incidents was a crime ultimately recorded by the police.) It seems that when the police responded to reports of disturbances, in both urban and rural areas, they most frequently ended up taking no official action. In many cases officers assessed the situation as having returned to normal by the time of their arrival or, if action was needed, they proceeded to take unofficial action such as giving advice or 'moving on' trouble-makers. In other words, the police tended to see their role when responding to such reports, as one of defusing the disturbance, if it was still continuing, rather than one of strict law enforcement.

Other reasons for public calls to the police included noise 'pollution', different types of nuisance, vagrancy and minor disturbances. Many of these incidents did not involve any breach of the criminal law and therefore formal action by the police would have been inappropriate. Nevertheless, an informal response was still possible in many cases, which again tended to involve giving advice or attempting to quieten down either the complainant or the object(s) of their complaint. So it seems that even in the case of relatively trivial public reports of incidents the police tended to respond by dispatching an officer to the scene of the incident. But, it was only in relation to fairly clear instances of criminal offences, especially property crime, that the police responded by taking formal action. In other instances, they were content to maintain (or restore) the peace.

By studying the content of the public's crime reports to the police, the researchers were able to assess whether there was any foundation to traditional views that rural crime follows a pattern which is qualitatively different from that which occurs in more densely populated areas. They found no justification for such views: 'the types of problems and crimes affecting residents and business people seemed to be similar in towns and villages.'[46] They found greater variation, in this respect, between the two urban police areas which they studied than between the rural and the urban areas. There were, of course, considerable *quantitative* differences between urban and rural crime rates, but the types of crime and related incidents followed broadly similar patterns.

Respondents were also asked about the amount of crime in their area, and their views were found to be, broadly speaking, an accurate reflection of recorded crime rates. For example, in the village areas, nearly all residents estimated the crime rate as low or very low. (Over 50 per cent of village residents estimated that there was 'almost no crime' in their area and more than a third stated there was 'not much crime'.) Although urban residents tended to think that the crime rates were higher in their area (than their village counterparts), there were some interesting variations in perception. In the urban areas, it was the most affluent residents (in area 4) who thought that their crime rate was the highest, despite the fact that this area was not in the highest crime area when judged by recorded offences.

Fear of assault was not found to be a problem amongst village residents, but urban dwellers thought there was a greater possibility of being subjected to an attack in their area. Women were more likely than men to think that they might be the victims of violence. Generally, the researchers found that urban residents' views as to their likelihood of being assaulted were based less on local knowledge or direct experience than on second-hand information (such as media reports). Moreover, 'their perception of their personal risk was related to their views about how attractive they thought they were likely to be to potential violent offenders . . . their perception of their vulnerability seemed to be a facet of their suspiciousness of the world outside.'[47] In addition to asking respondents to assess their chances of being assaulted, they were also asked how safe they felt going out alone after dark. Generally speaking, levels of fear were found to be higher amongst urban residents. For example, around 13 per cent of village respondents felt unsafe, in contrast to almost one third of those in the urban areas.

It will be remembered that the findings of many of the regional crime surveys suggest strongly that the public would like to see more foot patrol officers in their area. Shapland and Vagg also asked respondents for their views on the type of policing they wanted and found that there was considerable demand for a *local* police officer who would be known to residents. It was felt by many respondents, particularly those in the urban areas, that they did not know the police officers who worked in their area. A greater level of satisfaction was evident amongst the villagers of Southton; two-thirds wished to see no change from the policing which they already received. It was found that, in Southton, the local officer was a village resident and was known to (or could at least be identified by) most residents. Thus it seems that respondents wished to see, above all, a strong local base to their policing with identifiable officers who have a knowledge of local affairs and concerns.

There was a clear perception on the part of respondents, except those in Southton, that the police did not provide a very visible presence in their area. In order to assess the accuracy of this perception, the researchers carried out their own observations (albeit for a fairly short period) and discovered that respondents' impressions were well founded and that police officers were rarely to be seen. So, despite much talk about 'area beat' or 'community' policing by the police themselves, it did not appear that these concepts represented the reality of policing in most of the areas covered by Shapland and Vagg's research. Respondents expressed an antipathy to mobile patrolling by the police, as it was both impersonal and fleeting. Instead, they preferred the idea of foot patrols and the reassurance of a physical presence, to maintain (and even symbolize) order as much as to deter or investigate crime. Yet, despite these criticisms by the public, the researchers found a generally high level of support for the police in all of the survey areas. This fairly high level of satisfaction with the police provides an interesting contrast to the findings of some of the regional surveys referred to earlier in this chapter.

The researchers also made the valid point that, if the police wish to use officers in a more 'local' or community style of policing, it should be remembered that this form of policing is a two-way process.[48] In other words, it is not simply a matter of the police setting the agenda. They must also respond to the wishes of the public in their area, even if this means paying greater attention to offences and behaviour which the police do not regard as particularly serious. Furthermore, police skill in relation to this type of work will need to be developed as a specialization in its own right.

Overall, the researchers provided an in-depth comparison of policing, which comprised both formal and informal law enforcement, in rural and urban communities. In doing so, Shapland and Vagg also challenged some widely held beliefs about the differing nature of crime and other problems in rural and urban areas. Although crime rates were much lower in rural areas, offences were generally of a similar nature to those of the urban areas. They detected little evidence of the impending 'demise of informal social control'[49] although it was found that, in general, urban residents were more reluctant to take action than their rural counterparts. It was suggested that the police were not sufficiently attuned to the public's views and priorities and that this was illustrated by the way in which officers were deployed. The researchers concluded:

At the level of problems that residents . . . express about what is happening in their area, accountability of whatever form at the district level will not suffice. There needs to be local accountability as well – a local accounting by the police of what they do about individual incidents and more persistent problems in the area . . . But the accounting also needs to be made jointly by police, other formal agencies, and local groups. Priorities need to be communicated, action reported and plans concocted together.[50]

5

The Aberystwyth Crime Survey

Introduction

A particular strength of the victimization survey methodology is that it enables crime in local areas to be studied in depth. Apart from official police records – which are incomplete – there is relatively little specific information about crime and victimization within a particular locality. As we have seen, this has been partly remedied by major regional studies, such as the Merseyside and Islington surveys. However, most local surveys are preoccupied with crime as an urban, or even an inner-city phenomenon, and they tell us little about crime, victimization and policing in less densely populated towns and rural areas. There is a considerable criminological and policing literature devoted to urban areas, but comparatively little material on the rural environment. (A notable exception is provided by the work of J. Shapland and J. Vagg, which is discussed fully in the previous chapter.)[1] Although British Crime Survey findings have suggested that there are marked differences between the crime rates of urban and rural areas, recent publicity has highlighted the extent (and fear) of crime in rural areas.[2] It has long been a concern of this writer that there is very little reliable or detailed information about rural crime, and there is a paucity of research in this area.

Accordingly, it was decided to conduct a victimization survey in Aberystwyth, a university town in mid-Wales, situated in a predominantly rural area.[3] In doing so, it was hoped to provide an interesting comparison with crime surveys of urban areas, as well as offering information to a variety of social and law enforcement agencies. For example, the survey's findings will enable the police to benefit from the specific information on reporting rates and reasons for non-reporting. Moreover, the findings of the survey may provide existing crime prevention initiatives with a more solid factual basis. In addition, there may be implications for housing and parking developments, and for the security and insurance industries. In short, it was intended that a rural crime survey should establish a more comprehensive picture of the local crime problem and a range of information on matters related to victimization. In doing so, it was hoped to make some contribution to the process of setting priorities and allocating resources. Information about the groups most at risk, and those most in fear of crime, may also prove to be of practical value in the search for solutions: for example, in initiating crime prevention programmes. A further attraction of such a survey lies in its potential role as a corrective to public and media conceptions about crime levels, trends and risks.

Methodology of the Survey

Interviewing was carried out for the Aberystwyth Crime Survey (ACS) by NOP Social and Political in June 1993. A total of 259 interviews were obtained after contacting 340 addresses taken systematically and unclustered from the electoral register. Allowing for empty addresses, this represents a final response rate of around 80 per cent, which is higher than the figure obtained by the British Crime Survey (BCS). The questionnaire used by the interviewers was a modified and shortened version of the BCS questionnaire, and up to three victim forms were completed, where appropriate, for respondents. The sample did not include institutional buildings (such as student halls of residence), but in all other respects it represents an accurate cross-section of the adult population (aged sixteen and over) of Aberystwyth.

Background Information about Respondents

The sample contains 108 men and 151 women, with eighty-seven in the 16–34 age range, sixty-two in the 35–54 group, and 107 respondents aged fifty-five and over. There are 139 respondents in social categories ABC1 and 119 in C2DE. There are 103 respondents who live in households of three or more persons, eighty-nine in households of two, with sixty-seven living alone. The sample includes thirty-eight students, and 102 people in employment, with 155 who either own or are buying their own house, forty-four council tenants and forty-seven who rent private accommodation. The total sample reveals that seventy-six respondents were victims of crimes covered by the survey within the fourteen-month period taken by the ACS. A total of 116 victim forms were completed.

Main Findings*

The Aberystwyth population, as represented by the sample taken by the ACS, is a stable, not a transient one. (Although Aberystwyth is a university town, the sample did not include student halls of residence.) It was found that 65 per cent of respondents have lived for ten years or more in the area (i.e. within fifteen minutes walk of the town), and just 7 per cent have lived in the area for less than a year. As might be expected from such a stable population, a high level of contentment was evident amongst respondents; 65 per cent are satisfied with living in the area, with a further 28 per cent being fairly satisfied. A mere 6 per cent feel dissatisfied with living in the area. In relation to feelings of neighbourliness, 38 per cent would say that they live in a neighbourhood in which people do things together and try to help one another, whereas 41 per cent describe their neighbourhood as one in which people 'go their own way'. A further 18 per cent think that their neighbourhood is a mixture of co-operation and individualism.

Respondents were asked about fear of crime, both in general and with regard to certain specific crimes. It was found that 39 per cent feel very safe walking alone in their area after dark, with 36 per cent feeling fairly safe, 17 per cent a bit unsafe, and 9 very unsafe (see table 5.1). It could be argued that, with 75 per cent of all respondents feeling safe, fear of crime is not much of a problem. But, with only just over one third of the sample feeling very safe, this cannot be too readily assumed. In contrast to 63 per cent of male respondents, only 21 per cent of female respondents feel very safe walking alone after dark. However, a further 42 per cent of female respondents feel fairly safe, with only 15 per cent feeling very unsafe. Fear of walking alone after dark is more evident in the age category fifty-five and over, with 36 per cent feeling either a bit or very unsafe.

Table 5.2 reveals that levels of fear are very low where respondents are alone in their own home: 66 per cent feel very safe, 28 per cent fairly safe, 4 per cent a bit unsafe, and only 1 per cent very unsafe. Although fewer women than men feel very safe (52 as opposed to 86 per cent), less than 10 per cent of female respondents feel unsafe, and only 2 per cent feel very unsafe. Once again, fear was more evident in the 55-and-over age group, but even here it was not excessive, with 7 per cent feeling a bit unsafe, and just 3 per cent very unsafe.

It was found that virtually half of all respondents are worried about having their homes broken into and something stolen (16 per cent are

---

*The tables referred to in the following discussion can be found in the Appendix, starting on p. 127.

very worried, with 32 per cent fairly worried). Student respondents are the least worried about this, and council tenants are the most worried with 23 per cent very worried and 41 per cent fairly worried. Fear of being robbed and mugged is less common: for all respondents, only 15 per cent are very worried, with 22 per cent fairly worried. Fear of this type of crime is much more common amongst female respondents (20 per cent are very worried and 26 per cent are fairly worried), and amongst those aged 55 and over. Once again, the group of respondents most fearful are council residents – over half of this group are worried about being mugged and robbed.

For those to whom the question applied, just under half of all respondents are worried about their car being stolen, with men slightly more worried than women. Those who own or are buying their own home are more worried about this type of crime than those respondents who live in rented accommodation, whether this is private or council-owned. Overall, respondents are as worried about having things stolen from their cars as they are about having their cars stolen. It is perhaps surprising that people are not more worried about thefts *from* vehicles than they are about thefts *of* their vehicles.

Table 5.3 deals with worry about being raped. Over half of the female respondents are worried, with 29 per cent very worried, and 23 per cent fairly worried. Women in the 16–35 age group are more worried than older respondents. Women who live in council property are particularly worried about rape, with 51 per cent very worried, and a further 11 per cent fairly worried. In fact, the percentage of women in this category who are very worried is significantly higher than for any other group of respondents. However, students seem to be the most worried group, overall, in relation to this offence: 90 per cent expressed some worry about it and none of the student respondents described themselves as 'not at all worried'.

There is evidence, from successive sweeps of the British Crime Survey, of a decline in public confidence in the police during the 1980s.[4] This trend was widespread and did not simply apply to groups who were usually thought to be antagonistic towards the police. For example, the 1988 sweep of the BCS suggested that there had been a particular decline in confidence in the police in small towns and rural areas, and also in relation to elderly and female respondents.[5] As a recent commentator observed:

This trend was significant because the police depend on the co-operation of the public. The police rely on victims to report crimes quickly and accurately, and rely on witnesses coming forward to help the police investigate those crimes. The police also rely on the public to report accidents and emergencies.

In turn, the public expects effective and courteous service from the police . . .[6]

The 1992 sweep of the BCS suggested that public confidence in the police was still falling, but no further decline was evident in 1994. It is interesting to note the findings of the Aberystwyth survey in this context. They do not make reassuring reading for the police. Only 16 per cent of all respondents are prepared to say that the police do a very good job, and 48 per cent think that they do a fairly good job (see table 5.4). In a small town which enjoys a low recorded crime rate and a considerable spirit of local co-operation, it is surprising that public confidence in the police is not higher. In relation to public dissatisfaction, 14 per cent of respondents think the police do a fairly poor job, whilst 6 per cent say they do a very poor job, and 15 per cent do not know. Most surprisingly, it is the 55-and-over age group which is the least satisfied with the performance of the police. There is little overall difference in satisfaction levels between different social classes, but council tenants are less happy with the job done by the police than other groups. Those who have been recent victims of crime are less satisfied with the police than those respondents who have not been victims.

More than half of all respondents think that crime has increased over the last two years; 22 per cent think there is now a lot more crime, and 32 per cent a little more crime, with 35 per cent thinking that the crime rate is about the same as two years ago. Women are more likely than men to feel that crime is on the increase. Council residents are also more likely than other groups to think that crime is on the increase.

A mere 13 per cent of all respondents believe that there is a Neighbourhood or Home Watch scheme currently operating in their area, with 66 per cent stating that there is no such scheme in theirs. Surprisingly, 20 per cent do not know whether there is such a scheme in their area. The groups which appear to be the most unsure about the existence of these schemes are students (53 per cent don't know), the 16–34 age group (39 per cent don't know) and those living in privately rented accommodation (49 per cent don't know). It also appears that Home Watch schemes are more common in areas where people own their own homes (17 per cent), than in council owned areas (11 per cent), or in privately rented areas (2 per cent). But, the numbers here might be distorted by the high percentage of people who do not know whether a scheme operates in their area. Of those respondents who report that there is such a scheme in their area, 53 per cent say that their household is an active member of the scheme, 35 per cent say that their household is not, and 12 per cent do not know. Active membership of these schemes is more common in the 55-and-over age group (61 per cent), than it is in the younger age groups. Two-thirds of those whose homes are not in an area where a scheme currently operates say that they would join if one were set up.

Aberystwyth residents do not appear to be troubled by problems with noisy neighbours or loud parties. A mere 4 per cent find such noise a very big problem, and a further 7 per cent find it a fairly big problem. Similarly, the majority of people are not very troubled by teenagers hanging around on the streets in their area, or by drunks and tramps. However, 14 per cent find loitering teenagers a fairly big problem, and 9 per cent are fairly troubled by drunks and tramps on the streets. Those living in privately rented accommodation are more troubled by loitering teenagers, drunks and tramps than are those who live in either council property or houses which they own. Just under one third of all respondents are troubled by rubbish and litter lying about in their area and slightly fewer people are troubled by vandalism, graffiti and damage to property. Just 2 per cent of all respondents think that racially motivated attacks are a big problem in their area, whereas 14 per cent think that drug users are a big problem. Once again, it is residents living in privately rented accommodation who are more likely to find racial attacks and drug use a big problem in their area.

Tables 5.5–10 provide background information about the respondents, in terms of home ownership, gender, age, occupation and social class. These tables were summarized briefly at the start of this chapter. It was also established which respondents owned or regularly used a motor vehicle or motorcycle during the period covered by the survey. Of those who had such a vehicle, 99 per cent did not have it stolen or taken without permission during the fourteen-month period covered by the survey (hereafter the 'survey period'), and the 1 per cent who had their vehicle taken, suffered this victimization on one occasion only. No respondent had his or her vehicle taken or stolen on more than one occasion. It appears that theft from, or off, vehicles is a more common occurrence, with 6 per cent of respondents having suffered this once during the survey period, 2 per cent having suffered it twice, and 1 per cent being victimized three or more times. Overall, however, 92 per cent were not victims of this offence. Respondents in the 16–34 age group were more likely to have suffered this type of offence. In view of the unlikelihood of an Aberystwyth resident having his or her motor vehicle stolen, it is perhaps surprising that so many respondents are worried about this type of crime.

Vandalism to vehicles and damage to them caused by would-be thieves is a more prevalent crime in the area, with 13 per cent of vehicle owners having suffered this once during the survey period, 3 per cent having suffered it twice, and 2 per cent three or more times. Younger people are significantly more at risk, with over 30 per cent in the 16–34 age group having been victims of vandalism or damage to their vehicles, in contrast with the fifty-five and over group of whom just 11 per cent were victims of this crime. It would seem that students' vehicles are particularly vulnerable, with 35 per cent of student vehicle owners being victims. Those living in privately rented accommodation are also more at risk of this type of crime than either residents of council property or those who own their own homes. Obviously, chances of a car being damaged by vandals will increase where there is no private or secure parking for residents' vehicles. Of those respondents who own bicycles, only 2 per cent had them stolen during the survey period.

The survey looked specifically at those respondents who moved to their present address during the survey period; that is, 14 per cent of all the respondents in the survey (hereafter referred to as 'movers'). The majority of movers (78 per cent) moved to the area from a previous address which was no more than twenty miles away (with 60 per cent moving no more than two miles). Movers were then asked about specific crimes committed against them and their property during the survey period *before* they moved to their present address, with the following results: 11 per cent were victims of burglary, 3 per cent were victims of a break-in with damage, 3 per cent suffered an attempted burglary, no one had anything stolen out of their house of flat, nor did anyone have milk taken from outside, and 5 per cent suffered vandalism to their property. In the time covered by the survey period *since* the movers had been at their present address, none were victims of burglary.

The survey found that, of those respondents who lived at their present address throughout the survey period (i.e. 'non-movers'), only 1 per cent were victims of burglary, and no respondent was burgled more than once. All respondents were then asked about other specific offences committed against them at their present address: one respondent was a victim of a break-in with damage, 3 per cent were victims of attempted burglary, 1 per cent were victims of theft of property from their home, 6 per cent had milk stolen from outside, 5 per cent suffered other thefts from outside their homes (e.g. from gardens or garages), and 2 per cent were victims of vandalism to their homes or anything outside. No respondent was the victim of having anything which they were carrying, or anything from their pockets or a bag, stolen from them. Just one respondent was the victim of an attempted theft of this type. A mere 4 per cent of respondents were victims of other thefts of their property (e.g. from a cloakroom, or office), and around 2 per cent suffered vandalism or deliberate damage to their property.

It was further disclosed that approximately 4 per cent of all respondents were assaulted or were victims of violence during the survey period. Nearly all assault victims (with only one exception) were within the 16–34 age group and none were in the 55-and-over age group. A further 2 per cent of all respondents were threatened with violence or damage to their property. During the survey period, just 1 per cent of female respondents were sexually assaulted or attacked. The survey also looked at the incidence of domestic violence between members of the same household during the survey period. (This conduct covers assault with fists or a weapon, kicking, or any other violence.) Of all respondents living with another adult (aged sixteen or over) in the same household, 93 per cent said they had not been the victim of such violence, but only 89 per cent of women, and 86 per cent of those in the 16–34 age group, could say the same. Although no instances of domestic violence were reported directly to interviewers, there was quite a high 'no response' rate. In the 16–34 age group, 14 per cent gave no response to the question. As people in this age group were more likely than in any other group to have other people present at the time of the interview, it can be reasonably inferred that domestic violence was not uncommon in a number of these households, but that the lack of privacy of the interview made a candid response difficult.

During the survey period, just over 70 per cent of respondents did not suffer any of the offences covered by the survey, and around 30 per cent were victims (see table 5.11). There was no significant difference in the victimization rate according to gender, but the most frequently victimized groups were the 16–34 age group (43 per cent were victims, as opposed to just 17 per cent of those in the fifty-five and over age group), and students (47 per cent were victims). Respondents living in property rented from the council were less frequently victimized than either those renting privately, or those who own their own homes. Of those respondents who suffered a particular offence more than once, 90 per cent thought that the incidents were very similar ones, where the same thing was done under the same circumstances and probably by the same people.

Victims were then asked more specific questions about their experiences and a victim form was completed for each *single* incident. Any series of similar incidents counted as one incident (i.e. one victim form), but two or more *different* incidents of the same type each qualified for a separate victim form (up to three victim forms per person were completed). A total of 116 victim forms were completed for the Aberystwyth Crime Survey; the results of these are summarized below.

Experience as Victims (All Victim Forms)

Table 5.12 shows that damage and vandalism to vehicles was much more common than any other offence, accounting for 26 per cent of all incidents. The next most common offences were thefts from vehicles, thefts from outside houses (excluding milk bottles) and other thefts. In total 38 per cent of all offences recorded by the survey were in relation to vehicles or conveyances. Only 17 per cent of incidents involved offences against the person, such as assault or threats, but it should be remembered that a significant number of respondents did not answer the question about domestic violence in a direct manner. If a reliable figure for this type of offence could be obtained, there might possibly be a considerable increase in offences against the person recorded. Young people, particularly men, were more likely to be assaulted than any other group. This is consistent with the British Crime Survey findings discussed in chapter 3.

Ninety per cent of incidents recorded by the victim forms occurred in or around Aberystwyth, with the weekend being the most common time for an offence to have been committed. Approximately three-quarters of all offences were committed either during the evening or at night. The offences occurred in the victims' own homes in 24 per cent of cases, but in only half of these incidents did the offender actually get inside the property.

Just over a third of all victims were able to say something about the offenders, such as how many there were or the sort of people they were. Of those who could provide such information, 52 per cent said there was just one offender involved in their incident, 21 per cent thought that there were two offenders, and 21 per cent said there were three or more offenders. Where the characteristics of offenders could be identified by victims, they were found to be young, with 17 per cent of school age and 62 per cent between sixteen and twenty-five years old; they were also identified as being male in 83 per cent of cases and female in just 7 per cent of incidents. (In a further 5 per cent of cases, some of the offenders were male and some were female.) Where the victim could supply information about the offender(s), at least one of the offenders was known to the victim, before the incident, in around half of all cases.

Out of the 116 incidents recorded on the victim forms, 43 per cent involved something belonging to the respondent, or a member of his or her household, being stolen. Items most commonly stolen were car parts and accessories, clothes, and money (including purses, credit cards etc.). Items stolen varied considerably in value: in around a quarter of theft cases, the property was worth less than £10; in 40 per cent of cases it was worth between £11 and £50; in 12 per cent of incidents it was worth between £51 and £100; and in 18 per cent of cases, the property was valued at over £100. In the very small number of cases where a vehicle was stolen, it was recovered within twenty-four hours.

In 38 per cent of all incidents recorded on the victim forms, the offender either defaced or caused damage to property belonging to the victim or a member of the victim's household. In incidents where damage did occur, 23 per cent of cases involved damage of a total value in excess of £100, and 18 per cent involved damage totalling between £51 and £100. Of all respondents who had any property either stolen or damaged, 58 per cent said that the property in question was not covered by an insurance policy, 34 per cent stated that it was covered, and 8 per cent did not know. Where the property was insured, it is surprising that only 23 per cent made a claim on their policy. Presumably this reflects the relatively low value of much of the property which was stolen or damaged, and the terms of most insurance policies which require the insured to pay for the first part of any loss actually suffered.

Eight per cent of all victims thought that they themselves were in some way responsible (apart from the offenders) for what happened, because of something they did or forgot to do. A further 2 per cent thought that another member of their household was in some way responsible, apart from the offender, for what happened. However, the majority of victims (86 per cent) felt that they were not responsible in any way for the incident. Where victims did feel that they or other household members were in some way responsible, no clear pattern emerged as to the conduct which they thought had led to the incident, although 20 per cent thought that the offender had been provoked. It seems that very few offences resulted from the victim's failure to lock doors or windows, or as a result of property being left on display. It may well be that there *were* more cases of carelessness by victims, but that these were not admitted by respondents for a variety of reasons (such as embarrassment, or because of an insurance claim).

It was found that 73 per cent of victims were not aware of the offence at the time that it was happening. Of those who were aware, 83 per cent said that the offender did not have a weapon, or anything which was used or threatened as a weapon, with him. However, in those cases where victims were aware of what was happening, 53 per cent said that the offender used force or violence on someone. (It should be noted that this represents quite a small proportion of the *total* number of victims in the survey.) Where force or violence was used by the offender, it was directed towards the respondent in 94 per cent of cases. These acts of violence led to injuries in about two-thirds of the cases where force was used on the victim, but serious physical injury was very rare. Most injuries inflicted were cuts, bruises, 'black eyes', and scratches.

Overall, only 2 per cent of all victims covered by the survey received attention from a doctor as a result of the offence, and none had to stay overnight in hospital. However, 61 per cent of all victims said that the incident caused either themselves or a member of their household to have some kind of emotional reaction. The most common emotional reactions, amongst those who were so affected, were anger (in about 85 per cent of cases), shock (in about 30 per cent of cases) and fear (in about 15 per cent). A smaller number of affected victims said that the incident led to crying episodes and, in a few cases, difficulty in sleeping. Where the respondent had an emotional reaction to the offence, 28 per cent said that it affected them very much, 22 per cent 'quite a lot', and 47 per cent 'just a little'.

Interestingly, the police came to know about the crimes revealed by the survey in only 45 per cent of cases. Incidents involving male victims, or victims in the 16–34 age group, were less likely to come to the attention of the police. (Incidents revealed by male respondents on the victim forms showed that in only 32 per cent of cases did the police come to know about the offence.) A variety of reasons were given for not reporting the incident to the police, but the most common reason given (in around half the cases) was that it was too trivial to be worth reporting (see table 5.13). The next most common reason (in 13 per cent of non-reporting cases) was that the police could not have done anything about the incident. Men were more likely than women to want to deal with the matter themselves, but even amongst men this was not a common response to the offence. Dislike or fear of the police was given as a reason by only 5 per cent of 'non-reporting' victims, but 5 per cent also thought that the police would not have been interested in or bothered about the incident.

Where the police were notified about the incident, this was due to being informed by the respondent in 46 per cent of cases, being told by another person in the respondent's household in 27 per cent of cases, or being told by some other person (in 19 per cent of cases). The police were present when the incident occurred in one case only. Of all cases where the police were informed about the offence, 21 per cent of respondents said that neither they nor any other member of their household had any face-to-face contact with the police about the incident. However, in most cases where there was no face-to-face contact with the police, the respondent felt that such contact was not really necessary.

In cases where the police were informed, 67 per cent of respondents were satisfied with the amount of interest shown by the police in the reported incident. However, 23 per cent felt that the police showed less interest than the respondent thought they should have done, and a further 10 per cent were not sure (see table 5.14). The majority of reported incidents were dealt with promptly, with relatively few respondents complaining that they had to wait an unreasonable amount of time (only 6 per cent of cases), or that the police failed to attend to the matter (also in 6 per cent of reported incidents). A quarter of reported incidents did not result in a police investigation, but in those that did, victims were more likely than not to be dissatisfied with the amount of information they were given by the police about the progress of their investigation. (In all cases where the police were notified, only 17 per cent of victims thought that they were very well informed, and 8 per cent fairly well informed, about the progress made.) But, overall, in cases reported to the police, 35 per cent of respondents were very satisfied with the police's handling of the matter and 31 per cent were fairly satisfied, with 15 per cent a bit dissatisfied, and 10 per cent very dissatisfied (see table 5.15). For the majority of victims who reported their incidents, the resulting contact with the police made no difference to their view of the police, but for 15 per cent it led to a more favourable view of them, and for 10 per cent, a less favourable one.

Where the police were informed of the incident, they found out the identity of the offender in just 20 per cent of cases, and failed to do so in 54 per cent of cases. (A number of respondents were not sure.) Where the police did find out 'who did it', the victim was told by the police what happened to the offender in 40 per cent of cases. In cases where the police did become involved, as a result of the crime being reported, only 12 per cent of victims said that they were given any information about claiming compensation, in contrast to 67 per cent who said that they were not given any such information (with 15 per cent unable to remember). Even allowing for lapses in memory or confusion, it would appear that victims could be more routinely provided with such information on this matter by the police. (It will be remembered that the Victim's Charter contains a statement of good practice for the police in relation to services for victims.)[7]

Three-quarters of all victims had heard of victim support schemes, and in 6 per cent of all the incidents disclosed to the survey the respondent was contacted by Victim Support. A further 6 per cent who were not contacted by a scheme member said that they would have found it helpful, but 83 per cent of victims said that they would not have found it helpful. Of the small number who were contacted by Victim Support, there was a mixed reaction as to how useful they found this contact.

When all the victims in the survey were asked to rate the seriousness of the crime committed against them (or a member of their household) on a scale from 0 to 20, 84 per cent assessed the crime in the 0–10 category, and 63 per cent placed it in the 0–5 category (see table 5.16). Nevertheless, for a small but significant number of victims the offence was seen as a serious, or even a very serious one. All victims were asked about what should have happened to the offender (if caught) and only 8 per cent thought that prison would have been appropriate. Receiving compensation, favoured by 27 per cent, seemed to be of greater concern to victims than wishing to see any punitive measure imposed on the offender. (For further details of the response to this question, see table 5.17.) These findings offer support for increasing the use of compensation orders by the courts, and for giving precedence to compensation where a fine is also imposed.

Comparison with Welsh Respondents in the British Crime Survey

Comparisons can be made between the ACS findings, and those of the British Crime Survey (BCS) 1992, in relation to the 290 Welsh respondents who formed part of the sample taken by the national survey in England and Wales. There were fourteen Welsh sample points used by the BCS: Wrexham, Caernarfon, Brecon and Radnor, Carmarthen, Ceredigion and Pembroke North, Newport East, Alyn and Deeside, Delyn, Gower, Merthyr Tydfil, Swansea East, Pontypridd, Newport West, and Cardiff Central. These were all non-inner-city sampling points; there were no Welsh inner-city areas included in the BCS.[8]

Many of the sample points taken in the national survey are very different, demographically and in other respects, from the Aberystwyth area. However, it is interesting to see how the findings from the two surveys compare for certain key questions, although the conclusions drawn from such comparisons must be expressed with caution. The questionnaires used, and periods covered, ensure that there is *some* consistency in methodology, but the weighting differences in the sampling should be borne in mind, as should the fact that the ACS sample was drawn from the electoral register not the Postcode Address File. It can be argued that such sampling differences are unlikely to affect the results significantly, but the possibility of distortion should be noted before any crude comparisons can be made.[9]

The first area of comparison is in relation to fear of crime in general and fear of specific crimes, in particular. Of ACS respondents, 39 per cent feel very safe walking alone in their area after dark, with 36 feeling fairly safe, 17 a bit unsafe, and 9 very unsafe. For Welsh BCS respondents the percentage results were: 22 very safe, 35 fairly safe, 31 a bit unsafe, and 11 very unsafe. Thus, fear for personal safety on the streets appears to be rather less of a problem to Aberystwyth residents than it is to those living in many other areas of Wales. On the other hand, there is little difference in the proportion of respondents in both surveys who feel very unsafe.

Where respondents are alone in their own homes at night, 66 per cent of the ACS sample feel very safe, 28 fairly safe, 4 a bit unsafe, and 1 very unsafe. In contrast, 41 per cent of Welsh BCS respondents feel very safe, 44 fairly safe, 11 a bit unsafe, and 4 very unsafe. Although fear for personal safety when at home is not a major problem to either sample, it does seem that with nearly 15 per cent of Welsh BCS respondents feeling unsafe, this represents quite a difference from the Aberystwyth findings.

In comparing levels of worry about specific crimes, for ACS respondents 16 per cent are very worried about having their home broken into and something stolen, 32 fairly worried, 37 not very worried and 14 not at all worried. The corresponding percentages for Welsh BCS respondents are: 28 very worried, 41 fairly worried, 26 not very worried, and 4 not at all worried. Fear of being burgled would therefore seem to be much less of a problem in Aberystwyth than in many other areas of Wales. This is also true in relation to fear of being mugged and robbed, where 15 per cent of ACS respondents are very worried about this, 22 fairly worried, 34 not very worried, and 28 not at all worried. Whereas 25 per cent of Welsh BCS respondents are very worried, 32 fairly worried, 31 not very worried and 11 not at all worried.

In relation to car theft, roughly the same proportion of respondents in each sample were not car owners (i.e. just over one third). In the ACS, 12 per cent are very worried about having their car stolen, 17 fairly worried, 16 not very worried and 17 not at all worried. In the BCS, 21 per cent of Welsh respondents are very worried, 21 fairly worried, 16 not very worried, and 6 not at all worried. Similarly, 10 per cent of ACS respondents are very worried about having things stolen from their cars, with 20 fairly worried, 16 not very worried and 16 not at all worried. For Welsh BCS respondents, the corresponding figures are: 18 per cent very worried, 23 fairly worried, 16 not very worried, and 7 not at all worried.

Worry about rape amongst female respondents is quite similar in both surveys, with 52 per cent of Aberystwyth respondents being either very or fairly worried, as compared to 60 per cent of Welsh BCS respondents. Twenty-one per cent of Aberystwyth respondents are not at all worried about being raped, in contrast to just 12 per cent of Welsh BCS women. Of course, this difference could reflect the fairly high number of women aged fifty-five and over in the Aberystwyth sample. It should be remembered that this age group showed slightly lower levels of worry about this particular offence than the younger age groups, especially those aged 16–34.

Levels of satisfaction with the job done by the police are broadly similar between Aberystwyth and Welsh BCS respondents. In the ACS, 16 per cent think the police do a very good job, 48 a fairly good job, 14 a fairly poor job, and 6 a very poor job. The corresponding figures for Welsh BCS respondents are 14 per cent very good, 41 fairly good, 16 fairly poor, and 10 very poor. There were a similar number of undecided respondents in each survey.

There are striking similarities between the two samples in the estimates of respondents about the crime rate in their areas. About 53 per cent of Aberystwyth respondents think that the crime rate has increased in the last two years, compared with approximately 57 per cent of Welsh BCS respondents who hold this opinion. The main difference is that only 22 per cent of the Aberystwyth sample think that there is now a lot more crime, in contrast to 36 per cent of the Welsh BCS sample.

Just 1 per cent of ACS respondents were victims of vehicle theft, as opposed to just over 5 per cent of Welsh BCS respondents. In relation to thefts from vehicles, the rate of victimization was broadly similar, with 92 per cent of Aberystwyth car-owning respondents having no such offence committed against them, as opposed to 88 per cent of Welsh BCS respondents. However, Aberystwyth respondents suffered a higher incidence of vandalism and damage to vehicles, with 19 per cent being victims, as opposed to 15 per cent of Welsh BCS respondents. Damage and vandalism to vehicles was by far the most common offence disclosed by the ACS. It can be suggested, tentatively, that in view of the comparison with other Welsh areas using BCS data, Aberystwyth does suffer a higher than average incidence of this type of crime for a non-inner city area.

For those respondents who lived at their present address for the whole of the survey period, only 1 per cent of ACS respondents were burglary victims, as compared with 2.3 per cent of Welsh BCS respondents. Incidents involving break-ins with damage were rare in both samples – with just one incident in the ACS sample and 2 in the BCS sample of Welsh respondents. Three per cent of ACS respondents were the victims of attempted burglary, as compared with 2 per cent of Welsh BCS respondents. Just over 1 per cent of respondents in each sample were victims of thefts from their houses or flats.

Comparison with Dyfed-Powys External Study of Policing

It is instructive to compare the Aberystwyth Crime Survey (ACS) findings with those of a survey commissioned by the Dyfed-Powys Police, carried out in the same year. The Dyfed-Powys Police Survey (DPPS) was devised by the police Quality Research section together with researchers from Swansea University. The DPPS sample was drawn from Aberystwyth, Ammanford, Brecon, Llanelli, Newtown, South Pembrokeshire, Preselli, and Carmarthen and it comprised a total of just over 1,000 respondents. Aberystwyth, which forms part of the Dyfed-Powys police area, provided one tenth of the overall sample. The comparisons which follow are between the Aberystwyth Crime Survey (discussed above) and the hundred Aberystwyth respondents taken by the DPPS.[10]

Aberystwyth respondents to the DPPS were asked to what extent they feel that their local police protect the community. One tenth thought that they were very well protected, and half felt that the police provided quite good protection. Just under a quarter felt moderately protected, and 15 per cent felt poorly protected. The 26–35 age group felt the least protected, and the over-36 group felt the best protected. Women felt better protected by the police than men, and those who speak Welsh felt less well protected than those who did not speak Welsh. It was also found that 20 per cent were very satisfied with the quality of service provided by the police, 66 per cent were satisfied, 13 per cent were dissatisfied, with 6 per cent expressing no view on the subject (just one respondent was very dissatisfied). Women respondents were generally more satisfied with the service provided by the police than were male respondents. The least satisfied group was the over 55 age group.

The ACS did not find quite such a high level of satisfaction amongst respondents (see earlier discussion). It found that 16 per cent of respondents thought the police do a very good job, 48 per cent thought they do a fairly good job, 14 per cent thought they do a fairly poor job, 6 per cent thought they do a very poor job, and 15 per cent did not know. The ACS also found that the 55-and-over age group were least satisfied with the performance of the police. However, in contrast to the DPPS findings, the ACS suggested that female respondents were slightly less satisfied with the work done by the police in the Aberystwyth area than their male counterparts. (It should be remembered that the ACS sample of 259 local residents was appreciably larger than the Aberystwyth section of the DPPS).

The questions in the two surveys relating to perception of crime rates were slightly different and are not directly comparable. But, bearing this warning in mind, the following results were obtained. Half of Aberystwyth respondents to the DPPS thought that violent crime has increased recently, but nearly half thought that the rate of such offending has not altered. However, 68 per cent of this sample believed that the burglary rate has increased recently, and only 27 per cent felt that it is unchanged. Three-quarters felt that car crime has increased and one quarter felt that it remained the same. (A mere handful of respondents were of the opinion that any of these three types of crime were actually decreasing in numbers).

In the ACS, respondents were asked how much the crime rate (in general) had changed in the preceding two years. It was found that 22 per cent thought there is now a 'lot more crime', 32 per cent a 'little more crime', and 35 per cent 'about the same'; 12 per cent 'did not know' and just one person thought that there was now less crime than two years earlier. The DPPS found that female Aberystwyth residents were slightly more likely to regard violent offences as on the increase, and significantly more likely to regard car crimes as more prevalent, but that there was no difference between male and female perceptions of the burglary rate. On the other hand, the ACS found quite a conspicuous difference in perception based on gender. Of the male respondents in the ACS, 45 per cent felt that there is now more crime than two years ago, as opposed to 59 per cent of female respondents.

The DPPS results suggested that Aberystwyth respondents appear to feel safer than respondents from other parts of the Dyfed-Powys police area. This would seem to be a realistic attitude in view of the generally low crime rate in Aberystwyth. As with many other regional surveys, the DPPS found quite high levels of dissatisfaction (i.e. 75 per cent) with the amount of 'foot patrol' policing. A greater degree of satisfaction was expressed in relation to the provision of mobile patrols (with 67 per cent of respondents being satisfied). Similar to the findings of the Merseyside Crime Survey, the DPPS found that respondents thought that the main priority which the police should follow is that of responding to emergencies. The next most important functions of the police, in the view of DPPS respondents, are preventing crime and detecting offenders. Overall, respondents thought that these tasks were being performed fairly well (or at least not badly), although around one fifth of respondents felt that the detection rate of the Dyfed-Powys police was poor. There was considerable satisfaction with the performance of this force in relation to emergency calls, however, with 65 per cent believing that this was done well and 28 per cent thinking it was done moderately well. (Just 5 per cent believed that police performance was poor in this respect.)

Some comparison is possible between the findings of the two surveys in relation to the amount of information given by the police to victims of crime. The ACS found that, in those cases where a reported incident led to a police investigation, victims were more likely than not to be dissatisfied with the amount of information that they were given by the police about the progress which was being made. But, overall, in ACS incidents which were reported to the police, around two-thirds of respondents were satisfied with the police's handling of the matter.

DPPS victims were asked about the performance of the police in providing feedback to them: less than one in five thought this was done well; just over a half thought it was done moderately, and almost a quarter thought it was done badly. So it would seem from both surveys that more attention should be given by the police to providing information or 'feedback' to victims. From earlier research, it has emerged very clearly that the provision of information for victims is a matter that requires greater priority.[11] This has led to the Home Office issuing a circular[12] aimed at getting the police and other criminal justice agencies to improve the way that victims are dealt with and kept informed (about 'their' incident). The Victim's Charter also states that 'the police should outline to the victim the investigatory process. They should aim to ensure that he or she is told of significant developments in the case particularly if a suspect is found, if he is charged or cautioned, if he is to be tried, and the result of his trial.'[13] The Charter also asks the police to consider how well they keep victims in touch with the course of proceedings – with a view to encouraging each force to improve 'its performance'.[14]

The Dyfed-Powys survey was not a victimization survey in the sense that this term has been used throughout this book. But, it has been seen how both local and national victimization surveys have come increasingly to study police–public interaction and public attitudes to the police.[15] So although the Dyfed-Powys survey was more concerned with the public's perception of the work done by the police, the police 'image' in the area and suggestions for improvements in the future, it is still of obvious interest to compare its findings with those of the Aberystwyth Crime Survey.

Conclusion

There is now a considerable interest in victimology among both criminal justice researchers and policy makers. Victimization surveys have been conducted on behalf of the governments of several countries and, in addition to the British Crime Survey programme, there have been a number of British surveys of urban and inner-city areas. The Aberystwyth Crime Survey of 1993 applied a similar methodology to a rural, less densely populated area of Britain. Its purpose was to improve the information about crime, victimization, and policing in rural areas. As we have seen, rural crime has been a relatively neglected area of victimization research. It must be conceded that the sample taken for the ACS was fairly small and this, inevitably, has some implications for the results of the survey. (For a discussion of crime survey methodology in general, see chapter 3.) But, despite this limitation, the survey provides an interesting insight into such matters as fear of crime, confidence in the police, rates of victimization, issues of crime prevention and victim support, and attitudes to punishment. In doing so, it illustrates the strength of the victimization survey methodology.

In order to measure changes in patterns of crime, it is of course necessary to repeat a survey at regular intervals. It is hoped that this will also be done in relation to Aberystwyth. If the survey is repeated, it will be possible to check the accuracy of police claims that the crime rate in Dyfed-Powys is falling. It was stated, for example, that recorded crime in Dyfed-Powys in 1994 fell by 14 per cent from the previous year.[16] It was also stated that there was a 6 per cent reduction in crime in the Aberystwyth police division[17] with a decrease in most categories of property crime. This is very encouraging news, but it must be emphasized once again that these figures are based on crimes reported to and recorded by the police. It will be interesting to see if a similar pattern emerges when the local victimization survey is repeated.

Notes

Notes to Chapter 1

[1] For a discussion, see P. Mayhew et al., *The 1992 British Crime Survey* (HMSO, 1993), Home Office Research Study 132, chapter 2.

[2] See W. G. Skogan, *Contacts between Police and Public: Findings from the 1992 British Crime Survey* (HMSO, 1994), Home Office Research Study 134.

[3] Ibid.

[4] See M. Hough and P. Mayhew, *The British Crime Survey* (1983), Home Office Research Study 76, p.1.

[5] See, for example, R. Kinsey et al., *Losing the Fight Against Crime* (Blackwell, 1986); Hough and Mayhew, op. cit.; A. K. Bottomley and C. Coleman, *Understanding Crime Rates: Police and Public Roles in the Production of Official Statistics* (Saxon House, 1981).

[6] See the *Observer*, 1 July 1990. Also see *Crime against retail and manufacturing premises: findings from the 1994 Commercial Victimisation Survey*, 1995, Home Office.

[7] For an interesting, but now rather dated, study of 'workplace' crime, see J. P. Martin, *Offenders as Employees* (Macmillan, 1962).

[8] For a useful examination of the subject, see J. Morgan and L. Zedner, *Child Victims: Crime, Impact and Criminal Justice* (Clarendon Press, 1992). A recent survey by the NCH Action for Children found that many children who witness domestic violence may suffer long-term psychological harm. Many women who are attacked by their partners reported that the incidents were witnessed by their children. Many of these children, in turn, became violent and aggressive, or suffered problems at school or other social difficulties.

[9] See Mayhew et al., footnote 1, *1992 British Crime Survey*.

[10] See R. Wright, 'A Note on Rape Cases' (1984) *Brit. Jo. Criminol.* 399.

[11] See Kinsey et al., op. cit., footnote 5, p.5.

[12] Reported in the *Guardian*, 4 July 1990.

[13] Tom White, director of NCH Action for Children, stated recently that domestic violence was the second most common violent crime reported to the police, and made up over 25 per cent of all reported violent crime. See the *Guardian*, 6 December 1994.

[14] See Hough and Mayhew, op. cit., footnote 4, p.12.

[15] Ibid., p. 1.

[16] R. Sparks et al., *Surveying Victims: A Study of the Measurement of Criminal Victimization* (Wiley, 1977).

[17] See S. McCabe and F. Sutcliffe, *Defining Crime: A Study of Police Decisions* (Oxford University Centre for Criminological Research, 1978), Oxford University Centre for Criminological Research, Occasional Paper no. 9.

[18] For a useful discussion, see G. Chambers and A. Millar, *Investigating Sexual Assault* (HMSO, Scottish Office, 1983).

[19] For a discussion, see D. Farrington and J. Gunn (eds.), *Reactions to Crime: The Police, Courts and Prisons* (Wiley, 1985).

[20] See T. Jones and J. Young, *Guardian*, 28 August 1989.

[21] See, for example, *Guardian*, 29 April 1993, in which it was reported that ministers claim 'big drop in crime rate rise'!

[22] In 1983, the recorded figure was 1,300.

[23] Fear of crime is assessed in chapters 3 and 4.

[24] For a good discussion see Andrew Rutherford, *Prisons and the Process of Justice* (Heinemann, 1984). But for a rather different, but equally useful, approach, see K. Pease, 'Cross-National Imprisonment Rates', *Brit. Jo. Criminol.* (1994) vol.34, Special Issue, 125.

[25] For a clear warning, see the report of the Helsinki Institute for Crime Prevention and Control, affiliated with the United Nations (HEUNI), *Criminal Justice Systems in Europe and North America*, K. Pease and K. Hukkila (eds.) (1990), 36–7.

[26] *Guardian*, 19 April 1994.

[27] In 1993, there were 689 homicides in the United Kingdom in contrast to 25,000 in the United States.

[28] See K. Pease and K. Hukkila, op. cit., footnote 25, 101–5 where the authors conclude that 'countries high on one type of crime [tend] to be high on others'.

[29] See *Guardian*, 4 November 1993, based on Home Office statistics.

[30] As reported in the *Observer*, 19 December 1993.

[31] See Commons Hansard, 4.11.93, cols. 371–5, and Commons Hansard, 26.11.93, cols. 231–8. Also see the Labour Party's report *Everyone's a Victim* (1995).

[32] In 1993, the Prime Minister stated: 'It is in the inner cities that vandalism is rife . . . It is here that fear of violent crime makes a misery of old people's lives.'

[33] For example, see the report of the Employment Policy Institute (1995), written by John Wells, which suggested a close correlation between unemployment and recorded crime.

[34] The government announced its intention, in 1994, to go ahead with a national network of secure training centres for persistent juvenile offenders at a cost of £100 million.

[35] *Social Focus on Children* (HMSO, 1994).

[36] The number of 10–16-year-olds found guilty of offences or cautioned fell in England and Wales from 214,300 in 1981, to 139,900 in 1992: Source: Central Statistical Office's *Social Focus on Children* (HMSO, 1994).

[37] See *Guardian*, 6 July 1994.

[38] Source: *Guardian*, 6 July 1994.

[39] For a good discussion, see K. Bottomley and K. Pease, *Crime and Punishment: Interpreting the Data* (Open University Press, 1986), 42–9.

[40] See J. Burrows and R. Tarling, *Clearing Up Crime* (HMSO, 1982), Home Office Research Study No.73.

[41] See Kinsey et al., op. cit., footnote 5, 24.

[42] See *Guardian*, 31 January 1994.

[43] The figures for 1993 had not been published at the time of writing, and some of the clear-up rates for certain areas cover just part of 1993.

Notes to Chapter 2

[1] For a good, broad historical account of the different criminological theories and their development, see the seminal work of H. Mannheim, *Comparative Criminology* (Routledge, 1965), two volumes.

[2] See H. J. Eysenck, *Crime and Personality* (Paladin, 1964).

[3] See *Outsiders* (Macmillan, 1963), and the later edition with an additional chapter (1973), entitled 'Labelling theory reconsidered'.

[4] Ibid., 3–4.

[5] For an interesting collection of essays which show the diversity of approach, see P. Rock and M. McIntosh (eds.), *Deviance and Social Control* (Tavistock, 1974); and S. Cohen (ed.), *Images of Deviance* (Penguin, 1971).

[6] For an excellent discussion, see D. Chapman, *Sociology and the Stereotype of the Criminal* (Tavistock, 1968).

[7] See E. Pizzey, *Scream Quietly or the Neighbours Will Hear* (Penguin, 1974).

[8] See, for example, S. Grace's *Policing Domestic Violence in the 1990s*, Home Office Research Study No.139 (HMSO, 1995). This research suggests that Home Office recommendations for improving the police response to domestic violence are not followed with any great consistency.

[9] H. Becker, *Outsiders*, op. cit., footnote 3, 179.

[10] See E. H. Sutherland, *White Collar Crime* (Holt Rinehart and Winston, 1949).

[11] See W. G. Carson, 'White Collar Crime and the Enforcement of Factory Legislation' (1970) 10 *Brit. Jo. Criminol.*, 383–98.

[12] See P. Wiles, 'Criminal statistics and sociological explanations of crime', in W. G. Carson and P. Wiles (eds.), *The Sociology of Crime and Delinquency in Britain* (Martin Robertson, 1971).

[13] For an excellent discussion, see Mike Maguire, 'Crime statistics, patterns, and trends: changing perceptions and their implications', in M. Maguire et al. (eds.), *Oxford Handbook of Criminology* (Oxford, 1994), 233–91.

[14] See R. Kinsey et al., *Losing the Fight Against Crime* (Blackwell, 1986), where the findings of the Merseyside Crime Survey were discussed. Statistically, the strongest indicator of whether a person will be stopped and searched is whether s/he has been a victim of crime.

[15] See T. Jones et al., *The Islington Crime Survey* (Gower, 1986); and Kinsey et al., op. cit., footnote 14.

[16] See J. Young, 'Risk of crime and fear of crime: a realist critique of survey-based assumptions', in M. Maguire and J. Pointing (eds.), *Victims of Crime: A New Deal?* (Open University Press, 1988).

[17] Once again, see the Merseyside and Islington surveys, for example, which are fully discussed in chapter 4.

[18] See R. Mawby and S. Walklate, *Critical Victimology* (Sage, 1994).

[19] See, for example, J. Sim et al., 'Introduction: crime, the state and critical analysis', in P. Scraton (ed.), *Law, Order and the Authoritarian State* (Open University Press, 1987).

[20] For a discussion, see C. Harding and L. Koffman, *Sentencing and the Penal System*, 2nd edn. (Sweet and Maxwell, 1995), chapter 3.

[21] See David Thomas, 'Why the Sentence Fits the Crime', *Guardian*, 22 March 1994.

[22] For a good discussion see Lucia Zedner, 'Victims', in Maguire et al. (eds.), op. cit., footnote 13, 1207–40.

[23] See P. Rock, *Helping Victims of Crime* (Clarendon Press, 1990).

[24] See J. Shapland et al., *Victims and the Criminal Justice System* (Gower, 1985).

[25] As this was prior to section 36 of the Criminal Justice Act 1988, there was no system of appeal by the prosecution against this unduly lenient sentence.

[26] Research on the incidence and reporting of sexual assaults is looked at in more detail in chapter 4

[27] Also see V. Binney et al., 'Refuges and Housing for Battered Women', in J. Pahl (ed.), *Private Violence and Public Policy* (Routledge, 1985).

[28] For a discussion, see Anna T., 'Feminist responses to sexual abuse: the work of the Birmingham Rape Crisis Centre', in Maguire and Pointing (eds.), op. cit., footnote 16.

[29] Ibid., 60.

[30] Estimates suggest that less than a third are reported.

[31] See Anna T., op. cit., footnote 28, 61.

[32] Ibid., 64–5.

[33] It resulted from the Metropolitan Police Working Party on Rape Investigation, 1985.

[34] For a good account of these developments, see C. Corbett and K. Hobdell, 'Volunteer-based services to rape victims: some recent developments', in Maguire and Pointing (eds.), op. cit., footnote 16, 47.

[35] See Rock, op. cit., footnote 23.

[36] See C. Holtom and P. Raynor, 'Origins of victims support philosophy and practice', in Maguire and Pointing (eds.), op. cit., footnote 16, 17.

[37] See M. Maguire and C. Corbett, *The Effects of Crime and the Work of Victim Support Schemes* (Gower, 1987), for a government-funded evaluative study.

[38] See Shapland et al., op. cit., footnote 24.

[39] For a full discussion, see the report of a NAVSS Working Party, chaired by Lady Ralphs, *The Victim in Court* (NAVSS, 1988).

[40] See J. Raine and R. Smith, *The Victim/Witness in Court Project: Report of the*

Research Programme (Victim Support, 1991). Also see the Royal Commission on Criminal Justice (1993), Cm. 2263, paras. 36–40.

41 Royal Commission on Criminal Justice (1993), paras. 36–40.

42 *Compensation for Victims of Crimes of Violence* (Cmnd. 2323) (HMSO, 1964).

43 For a criticism of the narrow scope of the scheme, see D. Miers, *Responses to Victimisation* (Professional Books, 1978).

44 Council of Europe (1983).

45 For a good discussion of this issue, see A. Ashworth, 'Punishment and Compensation: Victims, Offenders and the State' (1986) 6 OJLS 86.

46 See D. Miers, op. cit., footnote 43.

47 Op. cit., footnote 42.

48 See T. Newburn, *The Settlement of Claims at the Criminal Injuries Compensation Board*, Home Office Research Study No.112 (HMSO, 1989).

49 See *R. v. Secretary of State for the Home Department, ex parte Fire Brigade Union and Others* [1995] 2 All ER 244.

50 For a discussion, see Harding and Koffman, *Sentencing and the Penal System*, op. cit., footnote 20, chapter 1.

51 For example, H. L. A. Hart, *Punishment and Responsibility* (Oxford, 1968); A. Ross, *On Guilt, Responsibility and Punishment* (Stevens, 1975).

52 See Hart op. cit., footnote 51, 13.

53 Ibid., 3.

54 The wide discretion enjoyed by judges was derided as the 'cafeteria' system by Professor Andrew Ashworth: see, for example, his essay 'The Criminal Justice Act 1991', in C. Munro and M. Wasik (eds.), *Sentencing, Judicial Discretion and Training* (Sweet and Maxwell, 1992).

55 For a full discussion of the relevant literature, see Harding and Koffman, op. cit., footnote 20, and also A. Ashworth, *Sentencing and Criminal Justice* (Butterworths, 1992).

56 But for a cautionary comment on comparing the prison populations of different countries, see C. Nuttall and K. Pease, 'Changes in the use of imprisonment in England and Wales 1950–1991' [1994] *Crim. LR* 326; and K. Pease, 'Cross National Imprisonment Rates' (1994) 34 *Brit. Jo. Criminol.*, Special Issue, 116.

57 Cm. 965 (HMSO, 1990).

58 Ibid., p.2, para. 1.6.

59 Ibid., p.4, para. 1.15.

60 Ibid., p.6, para. 2.8.

61 For a useful guide to this legislation, see M. Wasik and R. Taylor, *Criminal Justice Act 1991* (2nd edn., Blackstone, 1994).

62 See A. Ashworth and B. Gibson, 'Altering the sentencing framework' [1994] *Crim. LR* 101.

63 For more detail, see Harding and Koffman, op. cit., footnote 20, chapter 3, and Ashworth, *Sentencing and Criminal Justice*, 1992.

64 For a discussion, see C. Kelk, L. Koffman and J. Silvis, 'Sentencing practice, policy and discretion', in P. Fennell et al. (eds.), *Criminal Justice in Europe* (Clarendon Press, 1995).

65 Op. cit., footnote 57, para. 4.25.
66 For the relevant legislation, see the Powers of Criminal Courts Act 1973, sections 35–8, as amended by the Criminal Justice Acts of 1982 and 1988.
67 (1974) 60 Cr.App.R. 70.
68 See section 67, Criminal Justice Act 1982.
69 See T. Newburn, *The Use and Enforcement of Compensation Orders in Magistrates' Courts* (HMSO, 1988), Home Office Research Study No.102.
70 See D. Moxon, 'Use of compensation orders in Magistrates' Courts' (1993), *Home Office Research Bulletin* 25, and D. Moxon et al., *Developments in the Use of Compensation Orders in Magistrates' Courts since October 1988* (HMSO, 1992), Home Office Research Study No.126.
71 D. Moxon, op. cit., footnote 70, 29.
72 Also see the Victim's Charter (Home Office, 1990).
73 See Ashworth, *Sentencing and Criminal Justice*, op. cit., footnote 55, 250 where this point, *inter alia*, is well made.
74 For further discussion, see A. Ashworth, 'Punishment and compensation: victims, offenders and the state' (1986) *OJLS* 86.
75 See R. Barnett, 'Restitution: a new paradigm of criminal justice' (1978) 87 *Ethics* 279.
76 See *Bond* v. *Chief Constable of Kent* (1982) 4 Cr. App. R.(S) 314.
77 See section 35(4) Powers of Criminal Courts Act 1973.
78 See the comments of Lord Scarman in *Inwood* (1974) 60 Cr. App. R. 70 at 73. Also see *Bagga and Others* [1990] Crim. LR 128.
79 Per Lord Scarman in *Inwood* (1974) 60 Cr. App. R. 70 at 73.
80 For affirmation of this important principle, see *Barney* [1990] Crim. LR 209.
81 See Council of Europe Recommendation No.R (85) 11.
82 See Council of Europe Recommendation No.R (87) 21.
83 See D. Miers, 'The responsibilities and the rights of victims of crime' [1992] 55 Mod. LR 483; and J. Morgan et al., 'Protection of and compensation for victims of crime', in P. Fennell et al. (eds.), *Criminal Justice in Europe* (1995), 120–35.
84 Council of Europe, op. cit., footnote 82.
85 26 August–6 September 1985.
86 See R. Schaaf, 'New international instruments in crime prevention and criminal justice' [1986] 14 *International Journal of Legal Information*, 176.
87 See UN Declaration of Basic Principles of Justice for Victims of Crime and Abuse of Power, 1985, Article 6.
88 See *Victim's Charter: A Statement of the Rights of Victims of Crime* (Home Office, 1990).
89 Ibid., 9.
90 Ibid., 9–21.
91 See J. Plotnikoff and R. Woolfson, *Prosecuting Child Abuse* (Blackstone, 1995).
92 By the NCH Action for Children.

Notes to Chapter 3

1 See R. Lehnen and W. Skogan (eds.), *The National Crime Survey: Working Papers*, vol.1 (US Department of Justice, 1981).
2 See 'A chronology of National Crime Survey developments', in Lehnen and Skogan (eds.), op. cit., footnote 1.
3 S. Fienberg, 'Deciding what and whom to count' in R. Lehnen and W. Skogan (eds.), op. cit., footnote 1, 60.
4 See R. Dodge and A. Turner, 'Methodological foundations for establishing a national survey of victimization', in Lehnen and Skogan (eds.), op. cit.
5 These findings were based on pre-NCS tests conducted in Washington, DC (1970), Baltimore, Maryland (1970) and San Jose, California (1971). These 'pretests' are discussed further in Dodge and Turner's chapter, in Lehnen and Skogan (eds.), ibid.
6 See the National Research Council, 'The need for a continuing series of victimization surveys', in Lehnen and Skogan (eds.), op. cit., footnote 1.
7 Ibid.
8 See P. Mayhew and M. Hough, 'The British Crime Survey: origins and impact', in M. Maguire and J. Pointing (eds.), *Victims of Crime: A New Deal?* (Open University Press, 1988).
9 See R. Sparks, H. Genn and D. Dodd, *Surveying Victims* (Wiley, 1977); A. Bottoms et al., 'A localised crime survey in contrasting areas of Sheffield' (1987), *Brit. Jo. Criminol.* 125.
10 Mayhew and Hough, op. cit., footnote 8.
11 See M. Hough and P. Mayhew, *The British Crime Survey: First Report*, Home Office Research Study No.76 (HMSO, 1983).
12 For a fuller account, see Hough and Mayhew, ibid.
13 Ibid., 10.
14 Ibid., 16.
15 Ibid., 24.
16 For a detailed discussion of the BCS findings on fear of crime, see M. G. Maxfield, *Fear of Crime in England and Wales*, Home Office Research Study No.78 (HMSO, 1984).
17 For a fuller discussion of public attitudes to the punishment of offenders and the findings of survey research, see M. Hough and D. Moxon, 'Dealing with Offenders: Popular Opinion and the Views of Victims' (1985), 24 *Howard Jo.*, 160.
18 For a more detailed discussion of BCS findings on public attitudes to the police, see W. Skogan, *The Police and the Public in England and Wales: A British Crime Survey Report*, Home Office Research Study No.117 (HMSO, 1990).
19 See P. Mayhew and M. Hough, 'The British Crime Survey: origins and impact', in M. Maguire and J. Pointing (eds.), *Victims of Crime: A New Deal?*, 158.
20 See M. Hough and P. Mayhew, *Taking Account of Crime: Key Findings from the 1984 British Crime Survey*, Home Office Research Study No.85 (HMSO, 1985).

[21] See Hough and Mayhew, ibid., 16.

[22] For more detail, see K. Pease, *Judgement of Crime Seriousness: Evidence From the 1984 BCS*, Home Office Research and PU Paper 44 (HMSO, 1988).

[23] See Hough and Mayhew, op. cit., footnote 20, p.34.

[24] For all the relevant figures for reporting and recording rates found by the survey, see P. Mayhew et al., *The 1988 British Crime Survey*, Home Office Research Study No.111 (HMSO, 1989).

[25] Ibid., 16.

[26] For another study of ethnic minority perceptions of police performance and attitudes, see D. Smith and J. Gray, *Police and People in London* (Policy Studies Institute, 1985). Also see W. Skogan, *The Police and the Public in England and Wales: A British Crime Survey Report*, Home Office Research Study No.117 (HMSO, 1990).

[27] For an American study on this subject, see J. Lynch, 'Routine activity and victimization at work' (1987) *Jo. of Quant. Criminol.* 283.

[28] For further details, see Mayhew et al., 1989, op. cit., footnote 24, pp.41–50.

[29] On this subject, also see C. Brown, *Black and White Britain: The Third Policy Studies Institute Survey* (1984).

[30] See P. Mayhew et al., *The 1992 British Crime Survey*, Home Office Research Study No.132 (HMSO, 1993).

[31] Ibid., 18–19.

[32] See W. Skogan, *Contacts Between Police and Public: Findings From the 1992 British Crime Survey*, Home Office Research Study No.134 (HMSO, 1994).

[33] See, for example, the publication of the Victim's Charter: *A Statement of the Rights of Victims of Crime* (1990), Home Office.

[34] See Mayhew et al., op. cit., footnote 30, pp.42–4.

[35] For recent estimates of the victimization rates for burglary, see the *The General Household Survey 1993* (HMSO, 1994). This research was based on interviews conducted between April 1993 and March 1994 with 18,000 people.

[36] For further discussion, see D. Osborn et al., 'Area characteristics and regional variates as determinants of area property crime levels' (1992) 89 *Jo. of Quant. Criminol.* 265; and K. Pease, 'Individual and community influences on victimization and their implications for crime prevention', in D. Farrington et al. (eds.), *Integrating Individual and Ecological Aspects of Crime* (1993).

[37] For example, see G. Farrell, 'Multiple victimization: its extent and significance' (1992) 2 *Internat. Rev. of Victimology*, 85; G. Farrell and K. Pease, *Once Bitten, Twice Bitten: Repeat Victimization and its Implications for Crime Prevention* (1993), Police Research Group, Crime Prevention Unit Series Paper 46; and N. Polvi et al., 'The time course of repeat burglary victimization' (1991) 31 *Brit. Jo. Criminol.* 411.

[38] See R. Sparks, 'Multiple victimization: evidence, theory and future research' (1981) 72 *Jo. of Crim. Law and Criminol.* 762.

[39] See Mayhew et al., op cit., footnote 30, p.49.

[40] For a discussion, see Polvi et al., op. cit., footnote 37, p.414.

[41] See Mayhew et al., op. cit., footnote 30, pp.86–7.

[42] This figure is derived from 1988 and 1992 BCS data.

[43] For details of the survey, see *Trends in Crime: Findings from the 1994 Crime Survey*, P. Mayhew et al., Home Office Research and Statistics Department, Research Findings No.14, September 1994. Also see N. Aye Maung, 'The 1994 British Crime Survey', vol.51, *The Magistrate*, 1995, 35.

[44] For a very useful discussion, see P. Mayhew, 'Some methodological issues in victimization surveys', in *Crime Victims Surveys in Australia* (Conference Proceedings), Brisbane Criminal Justice Commission, 1995.

[45] Ibid., p.18.

[46] P. Mayhew et al., above, footnote 43, p.2.

[47] See M. Hough, *Anxiety about Crime: Findings from the 1994 British Crime Survey*, Home Office Research Study No.147 (HMSO, 1995).

Notes to Chapter 4

[1] For an interesting discussion, see M. Brogden et al., *Introducing Police Work* (Unwin Hyman, 1988), 181–90.

[2] *Police Watch* (October 1986).

[3] Ibid.

[4] Ibid.

[5] See *Police Watch* (July 1987), 7–10.

[6] Ibid., 9.

[7] Ibid., 10.

[8] See *Investigating Sexual Assaults* (HMSO, Scottish Office, 1983), 7.

[9] See E. Stanko, 'Hidden fears', *Guardian*, 5 September 1983; and E. Stanko, 'Hidden violence against women', in M. Maguire and J. Pointing (eds.), *Victims of Crime: A New Deal?* (Open University Press, 1988). Also see R. Hall, *Ask Any Woman* (Falling Wall Press, 1985).

[10] See *Crime in Newham: A Report of a Survey of Crime and Racial Harassment in Newham* (London Borough of Newham, 1987).

[11] For a discussion of 'encounters initiated by the police', based on BCS data, see W. Skogan, *Contacts Between Police and Public: Findings from the 1992 British Crime Survey*, Home Office Research Study No.134 (HMSO, 1994), pp.16–18.

[12] *Crime in Newham*, op. cit., footnote 29.

[13] Ibid., 30.

[14] Ibid., 42.

[15] Ibid., 43.

[16] For further discussion of police accountability issues, see J. Baxter and L. Koffman (eds.), *Police: The Constitution and the Community* (Professional Books, 1985), chapters 5, 6, 11 and 15; L. Lustgarten, *The Governance of the Police* (Sweet and Maxwell, 1986); and R. Reiner, *The Politics of the Police*, 2nd edn. (Wheatsheaf, 1992), chapter 6.

[17] See R. Kinsey, *Merseyside Crime Survey, First Report* (Liverpool Police Committee Support Unit, 1984).

[18] See Brogden et al., *Introducing Police Work*, op. cit., footnote 1, 183.

[19] For further details, see R. Kinsey, *Merseyside Crime and Police Surveys: Final Report* (1985).

[20] R. Kinsey et al., *Losing the Fight Against Crime* (Blackwell, 1986), 3.

[21] See R. Kinsey, *Survey of Merseyside Police Officers: First Report* (1985), 25–6.

[22] Ibid., 39.

[23] Ibid., 45–6 for further details.

[24] For similar findings, see the Policy Studies Institute study of the Metropolitan Police, *Police and People in London*, vol.III (1983), 38–40.

[25] See T. Jones et al., *The Islington Crime Survey* (Gower, 1986).

[26] Ibid., 1.

[27] Ibid., 4.

[28] For details of the methodology, see Jones et al., *Islington Crime Survey*, Appendix 2.

[29] See A. Crawford et al., *Second Islington Crime Survey* (Middlesex Polytechnic, 1990).

[30] Jones et al., *Islington Crime Survey*, op. cit., footnote 25, 45.

[31] Ibid., 109.

[32] This conclusion was reached by comparing the figures with those of the Policy Studies Institute's study, *Police and People in London* (Policy Studies Institute, 1983).

[33] Jones et al., *Islington Crime Survey*, op. cit., footnote 25, 157–8.

[34] Ibid., 160. Also see the findings of the 1988 Islington survey, in Crawford et al., *Second Islington Crime Survey*, op. cit., footnote 29, 44–58.

[35] Jones et al., ibid., 182.

[36] Ibid., 175.

[37] Ibid., 200.

[38] See, for example, M. Brogden et al., *Introducing Policework* (Unwin Hyman, 1988), 183–90. Also see J. Sim, P. Scraton and P. Gordon, 'Introduction: crime, the state and critical analysis', in P. Scraton (ed.), *Law, Order and the Authoritarian State* (Open University Press, 1987).

[39] Jones et al., *Islington Crime Survey*, op. cit., footnote 25, 6.

[40] For example, see recent interest in the development of a 'parish constable' scheme, as discussed in P. Hirst, 'Rebirth of the parish constable', in *Policing* (1994), 196–204.

[41] See *Guardian*, 8 December 1994.

[42] Ibid.

[43] See J. Shapland and J. Vagg, *Policing by the Public* (Routledge, 1988).

[44] Ibid., 19.

[45] Ibid., 39.

[46] Ibid., 43.

[47] Ibid., 117.

[48] Ibid., 151.

[49] Ibid., 174.

[50] Ibid., 192.

Notes to Chapter 5

[1] See J. Shapland and J. Vagg, *Policing by the Public* (Routledge, 1988).

[2] See chapter 1 for a discussion of recent criminal statistics.

[3] Aberystwyth is a small, seaside town with a population, excluding the student body, of about 12,000.

[4] See W. Skogan, *Contacts between Police and Public: Findings from the 1992 British Crime Survey*, Home Office Research Study No.134 (HMSO, 1994).

[5] Ibid., 5.

[6] Ibid., 5.

[7] See chapter 2 for a more detailed discussion of the position of victims in the criminal justice system.

[8] Source: Appendix A, to the British Crime Survey 1992: Technical Reports.

[9] For details of weighting in the British Crime Survey, see P. Mayhew et al., *The 1992 British Crime Survey*, Home Office Research Study No.132, (HMSO, 1993), 156–7.

[10] For further details, see *Extended Survey 1994*, Dyfed-Powys Police, unpublished survey by Opinion Research Service Ltd. and Headquarters Quality Support Department.

[11] For example, see T. Newburn and S. Merry, *Keeping in Touch: Police–Victim Communication in Two Areas*, Home Office Research Study No.116 (HMSO, 1990).

[12] See HOC 20/1988.

[13] See the Victim's Charter (Home Office, 1990), 9.

[14] Ibid., 22.

[15] For a recent study of these subjects, based on BCS data, see Skogan, *Contacts between Police and Public*, op. cit., note 4.

[16] Based on a report by the Dyfed-Powys Chief Constable, Raymond White, delivered to a police authority meeting, and reported in the *Cambrian News*, 13 January 1995.

[17] Ibid. It should be stressed that these were only provisional figures.

Appendix: Aberystwyth Crime Survey 1993

(Selected Tables)

TABLE 5.1

Q. How safe do you feel walking alone in this area after dark?

Base: All respondents

Figures in bold italic are percentages.

	Total	Sex		Age			Class		No. in household			Respondent		Police		Tenure			Victim	
		M	F	16-34	35-54	55+	ABC1	C2DE	1	2	3+	Works	Stud.	Good	Not good	Own/ buying	Coun.	Priv.	Yes	No
Total	259	108	151	87	62	107	139	119	67	89	103	102	38	166	93	155	44	47	76	183
Very safe (2)	100 *39*	68 *63*	32 *21*	38 *44*	21 *34*	40 *37*	59 *42*	40 *34*	24 *36*	38 *43*	38 *37*	42 *41*	17 *45*	69 *42*	31 *33*	61 *39*	14 *32*	19 *40*	26 *34*	74 *40*
Fairly safe (1)	92 *36*	29 *27*	63 *42*	30 *34*	32 *52*	29 *27*	49 *35*	43 *36*	22 *33*	25 *28*	45 *44*	42 *41*	15 *39*	59 *36*	33 *35*	55 *35*	15 *34*	17 *36*	28 *37*	64 *35*
A bit unsafe (−1)	43 *17*	10 *9*	33 *22*	14 *16*	7 *11*	21 *20*	18 *13*	25 *21*	10 *15*	18 *20*	15 *15*	12 *12*	6 *16*	27 *16*	16 *17*	23 *15*	9 *20*	9 *19*	14 *18*	29 *16*
Very unsafe (−2)	24 *9*	1 *1*	23 *15*	5 *6*	2 *3*	17 *16*	13 *9*	11 *9*	11 *16*	8 *9*	5 *5*	6 *6*	– –	11 *7*	13 *14*	16 *10*	6 *14*	2 *4*	8 *11*	16 *9*
All safe	192 *74*	97 *90*	95 *63*	68 *78*	53 *85*	69 *64*	108 *78*	83 *70*	46 *69*	63 *71*	83 *81*	84 *82*	32 *84*	128 *77*	64 *69*	116 *75*	29 *66*	36 *77*	54 *71*	138 *75*
All unsafe	67 *26*	11 *10*	56 *37*	19 *22*	9 *15*	38 *36*	31 *22*	36 *30*	21 *31*	26 *29*	20 *19*	18 *18*	6 *16*	38 *23*	29 *31*	39 *25*	15 *34*	11 *23*	22 *29*	45 *25*
Mean score	0.78	1.42	0.32	0.94	1.02	0.50	0.88	0.64	0.57	0.75	0.93	1.00	1.13	0.89	0.57	0.79	0.50	0.89	0.66	0.83

Key: Coun. = Council; F = Female; M = Male; Priv. = Private; Stud. = Student.

TABLE 5.2

Q. How safe do you feel when you are alone in your own home at night?
Base: All respondents

Figures in bold italic are percentages

	Total	Sex		Age			Class		No. in household			Respondent		Police		Tenure			Victim	
		M	F	16–34	35–54	55+	ABC1	C2DE	1	2	3+	Works	Stud.	Good	Not good	Own/buying	Coun.	Priv.	Yes	No
Total	259	108	151	87	62	107	139	119	67	89	103	102	38	166	93	155	44	47	76	183
Very safe (2)	171	93	78	57	48	64	89	81	45	56	70	74	25	117	54	104	28	30	45	126
	66	*86*	*52*	*66*	*77*	*60*	*64*	*68*	*67*	*63*	*68*	*73*	*66*	*70*	*58*	*67*	*64*	*64*	*59*	*69*
Fairly safe (1)	73	14	59	27	13	32	42	31	19	26	28	26	11	43	30	42	12	15	25	48
	28	*13*	*39*	*31*	*21*	*30*	*30*	*26*	*28*	*29*	*27*	*25*	*29*	*26*	*32*	*27*	*27*	*32*	*33*	*26*
A bit unsafe (-1)	11	1	10	3	1	7	6	5	2	5	4	1	2	5	6	7	3	1	5	6
	4	*1*	*7*	*3*	*2*	*7*	*4*	*4*	*3*	*6*	*4*	*1*	*5*	*3*	*6*	*5*	*7*	*2*	*7*	*3*
Very unsafe (-2)	3	-	3	-	-	3	1	2	1	1	1	1	-	-	3	1	1	1	1	2
	1	-	*2*	-	-	*3*	*1*	*2*	*1*	*1*	*1*	*1*	-	-	*3*	*1*	*2*	*2*	*1*	*1*
No response	1	-	1	-	-	1	1	-	-	1	-	-	-	1	-	1	-	-	-	1
	*	-	*1*	-	-	*1*	*1*	-	-	*1*	-	-	-	*1*	-	*1*	-	-	-	*1*
Mean score	1.54	1.84	1.33	1.59	1.74	1.39	1.54	1.55	1.57	1.49	1.57	1.68	1.55	1.65	1.35	1.56	1.43	1.53	1.42	1.59

Key: Coun.=Council; F=Female; M=Male; Priv.=Private; Stud.=Student.
*=less than .5

TABLE 5.3

Q. Most of us worry at some time or other about being the victim of a crime. Could you tell me how worried are you about being raped?
Base: All women

Figures in bold italic are percentages

	Total	Sex		Age			Class		No. in household			Respondent		Police		Tenure			Victim	
		M	F	16-34	35-54	55+	ABC1	C2DE	1	2	3+	Works	Stud.	Good	Not good	Own/ buying	Coun.	Priv.	Yes	No
Total	151	-	151	52	38	59	81	69	42	42	67	55	20	94	57	83	35	26	43	108
Very worried (2)	44 *29*	- -	44 *29*	17 *33*	11 *29*	16 *27*	21 *26*	23 *33*	14 *33*	10 *24*	20 *30*	15 *27*	6 *30*	26 *28*	18 *32*	18 *22*	18 *51*	7 *27*	15 *35*	29 *27*
Fairly worried (1)	35 *23*	- -	35 *23*	17 *33*	7 *18*	10 *17*	25 *31*	10 *14*	15 *36*	6 *14*	14 *21*	11 *20*	12 *60*	21 *22*	14 *25*	16 *19*	4 *11*	15 *58*	12 *28*	23 *21*
Not very worried (-1)	39 *26*	- -	39 *26*	15 *29*	11 *29*	13 *22*	16 *20*	23 *33*	4 *10*	13 *31*	22 *33*	18 *33*	2 *10*	28 *30*	11 *19*	25 *30*	7 *20*	3 *12*	9 *21*	30 *28*
Not at all worried (-2)	32 *21*	- -	32 *21*	3 *6*	9 *24*	19 *32*	19 *23*	12 *17*	9 *21*	12 *29*	11 *16*	11 *20*	- -	18 *19*	14 *25*	24 *29*	5 *14*	1 *4*	7 *16*	25 *23*
Not applicable	- -	- -	- -	- -	- -	- -	- -	- -	- -	- -	- -	- -	- -	- -	- -	- -	- -	- -	- -	- -
Don't know	- -	- -	- -	- -	- -	- -	- -	- -	- -	- -	- -	- -	- -	- -	- -	- -	- -	- -	- -	- -
No response	1 *1*	- -	1 *1*	- -	- -	1 *2*	- -	1 *1*	- -	1 *2*	- -	- -	- -	1 *1*	- -	- -	1 *3*	- -	- -	1 *1*
All worried	79 *52*	- -	79 *52*	34 *65*	18 *47*	26 *44*	46 *57*	33 *48*	29 *69*	16 *38*	34 *51*	26 *47*	18 *90*	47 *50*	32 *56*	34 *41*	22 *63*	22 *85*	27 *63*	52 *48*
All not worried	71 *47*	- -	71 *47*	18 *35*	20 *53*	32 *54*	35 *43*	35 *51*	13 *31*	25 *60*	33 *49*	29 *53*	2 *10*	46 *49*	25 *44*	49 *59*	12 *34*	4 *15*	16 *37*	55 *51*
Mean score	0.13	-	0.13	0.58	0.00	-0.16	0.16	0.13	0.50	-0.27	0.15	0.02	1.10	0.10	0.19	-0.25	0.68	0.92	0.44	0.01

Key: Coun.=Council; F=Female; M=Male; Priv.=Private; Stud.=Student.

TABLE 5.4

Q. Taking everything into account, would you say the police in this area do a good job or a poor job?
Base: All respondents

Figures in bold italic are percentages

	Total	Sex		Age			Class		No. in household			Respondent		Police		Tenure			Victim	
		M	F	16-34	35-54	55+	ABC1	C2DE	1	2	3+	Works	Stud.	Good	Not good	Own/ buying	Coun.	Priv.	Yes	No
Total	259	108	151	87	62	107	139	119	67	89	103	102	38	166	93	155	44	47	76	183
Very good (2)	42	19	23	11	8	22	28	14	10	14	18	14	6	42	-	26	4	9	7	35
	16	*18*	*15*	*13*	*13*	*21*	*20*	*12*	*15*	*16*	*17*	*14*	*16*	*25*	*-*	*17*	*9*	*19*	*9*	*19*
Fairly good (1)	124	53	71	49	36	37	59	64	37	32	55	55	20	124	-	69	21	26	42	82
	48	*49*	*47*	*56*	*58*	*35*	*42*	*54*	*55*	*36*	*53*	*54*	*53*	*75*	*-*	*45*	*48*	*55*	*55*	*45*
Fairly poor (-1)	37	13	24	10	9	18	17	20	4	15	18	16	2	-	37	26	9	1	14	23
	14	*12*	*16*	*11*	*15*	*17*	*12*	*17*	*6*	*17*	*17*	*16*	*5*	*-*	*40*	*17*	*20*	*2*	*18*	*13*
Very poor (-2)	16	8	8	6	2	8	9	7	3	9	4	6	2	-	16	12	2	2	8	8
	6	*7*	*5*	*7*	*3*	*7*	*6*	*6*	*4*	*10*	*4*	*6*	*5*	*-*	*17*	*8*	*5*	*4*	*11*	*4*
Don't know	40	15	25	11	7	22	26	14	13	19	8	11	8	-	40	22	8	9	5	35
	15	*14*	*17*	*13*	*11*	*21*	*19*	*12*	*19*	*21*	*8*	*11*	*21*	*-*	*43*	*14*	*18*	*19*	*7*	*19*
All good	166	72	94	60	44	59	87	78	47	46	73	69	26	166	-	95	25	35	49	117
	64	*67*	*62*	*69*	*71*	*55*	*63*	*66*	*70*	*52*	*71*	*68*	*68*	*100*	*-*	*61*	*57*	*74*	*64*	*64*
All poor	53	21	32	16	11	26	26	27	7	24	22	22	4	-	53	38	11	3	22	31
	20	*19*	*21*	*18*	*18*	*24*	*19*	*23*	*10*	*27*	*21*	*22*	*11*	*-*	*57*	*25*	*25*	*6*	*29*	*17*
Mean score	0.63	0.67	0.61	0.64	0.71	0.55	0.71	0.55	0.87	0.39	0.68	0.60	0.87	1.25	-1.30	0.53	0.44	1.03	0.37	0.76

Key: Coun.=Council; F=Female; M=Male; Priv.=Private; Stud.=Student.

TABLE 5.5

Home ownership
Base: All respondents

Figures in bold italic are percentages

	Total	Sex		Age			Class		No. in household			Respondent		Police		Tenure			Victim	
		M	F	16-34	35-54	55+	ABC1	C2DE	1	2	3+	Works	Stud.	Good	Not good	Own/buying	Coun.	Priv.	Yes	No
Total	259	108	151	87	62	107	139	119	67	89	103	102	38	166	93	155	44	47	76	183
Owned/being bought	155	72	83	28	44	81	89	65	21	69	65	72	3	95	60	155	-	-	49	106
	60	*67*	*55*	*32*	*71*	*76*	*64*	*55*	*31*	*78*	*63*	*71*	*8*	*57*	*65*	*100*	-	-	*64*	*58*
Rented from the council	44	9	35	15	13	16	6	38	12	11	21	17	2	25	19	-	44	-	6	38
	17	*8*	*23*	*17*	*21*	*15*	*4*	*32*	*18*	*12*	*20*	*17*	*5*	*15*	*20*	-	*100*	-	*8*	*21*
Rented privately	47	21	26	41	2	4	40	7	31	6	10	7	32	35	12	-	-	47	17	30
	18	*19*	*17*	*47*	*3*	*4*	*29*	*6*	*46*	*7*	*10*	*7*	*84*	*21*	*13*	-	-	*100*	*22*	*16*
Rented from a housing association	8	3	5	2	3	2	3	5	3	1	4	3	1	7	1	-	-	-	4	4
	3	*3*	*3*	*2*	*5*	*2*	*2*	*4*	*4*	*1*	*4*	*3*	*3*	*4*	*1*	-	-	-	*5*	*2*
Other	5	3	2	1	-	4	1	4	-	2	3	3	-	4	1	-	-	-	-	5
	2	*3*	*1*	*1*	-	*4*	*1*	*3*	-	*2*	*3*	*3*	-	*2*	*1*	-	-	-	-	*3*
Don't know	-	-	-	-	-	-	-	-	-	-	-	-	-	-	-	-	-	-	-	-
	-	-	-	-	-	-	-	-	-	-	-	-	-	-	-	-	-	-	-	-

Key: Coun.=Council; F=Female; M=Male; Priv.=Private; Stud.=Student.

TABLE 5.6

Number in household
Base: All respondents

Figures in bold italic are percentages

	Total	Sex		Age			Class		No. in household			Respondent		Police		Tenure			Victim	
		M	F	16-34	35-54	55+	ABC1	C2DE	1	2	3+	Works	Stud.	Good	Not good	Own/ buying	Coun.	Priv.	Yes	No
Total	259	108	151	87	62	107	139	119	67	89	103	102	38	166	93	155	44	47	76	183
1	67 *26*	25 *23*	42 *28*	32 *37*	8 *13*	25 *23*	45 *32*	22 *18*	67 *100*	– –	– –	17 *17*	23 *61*	47 *28*	20 *22*	21 *14*	12 *27*	31 *66*	21 *28*	46 *25*
2	89 *34*	47 *44*	42 *28*	11 *13*	12 *19*	66 *62*	43 *31*	45 *38*	– –	89 *100*		26 *25*	2 *5*	46 *28*	43 *46*	69 *45*	11 *25*	6 *13*	20 *26*	69 *38*
3	36 *14*	13 *12*	23 *15*	11 *13*	13 *21*	12 *11*	20 *14*	16 *13*	– –		36 *35*	21 *21*	1 *3*	23 *14*	13 *14*	25 *16*	6 *14*	1 *2*	14 *18*	22 *12*
4	39 *15*	12 *11*	27 *18*	16 *18*	21 *34*	2 *2*	16 *12*	23 *19*			39 *38*	27 *26*	3 *8*	28 *17*	11 *12*	25 *16*	10 *23*	2 *4*	8 *11*	31 *17*
5	20 *8*	6 *6*	14 *9*	11 *13*	6 *10*	2 *2*	9 *6*	11 *9*			20 *19*	9 *9*	4 *11*	14 *8*	6 *6*	13 *8*	4 *9*	3 *6*	11 *14*	9 *5*
6+	8 *3*	5 *5*	3 *2*	6 *7*	2 *3*	– –	6 *4*	2 *2*			8 *8*	2 *2*	5 *13*	8 *5*	– –	2 *1*	1 *2*	4 *9*	2 *3*	6 *3*
Mean score	2.54	2.46	2.59	2.78	3.18	1.97	2.42	2.68	1.00	2.00	4.00	2.91	2.42	2.64	2.35	2.65	2.68	1.98	2.66	2.49

Key: Coun.=Council; F=Female; M=Male; Priv.=Private; Stud.=Student.

TABLE 5.7

Respondent is . . . .
Base: All respondents

Figures in bold italic are percentages

	Total	Sex		Age			Class		No. in household			Respondent		Police		Tenure			Victim	
		M	F	16-34	35-54	55+	ABC1	C2DE	1	2	3+	Works	Stud.	Good	Not good	Own/ buying	Coun.	Priv.	Yes	No
Total	259	108	151	87	62	107	139	119	67	89	103	102	38	166	93	155	44	47	76	183
Male	108	108	-	35	24	48	58	50	25	47	36	47	18	72	36	72	9	21	33	75
	42	*100*	-	*40*	*39*	*45*	*42*	*42*	*37*	*53*	*35*	*46*	*47*	*43*	*39*	*46*	*20*	*45*	*43*	*41*
Female	151	-	151	52	38	59	81	69	42	42	67	55	20	94	57	83	35	26	43	108
	58	-	*100*	*60*	*61*	*55*	*58*	*58*	*63*	*47*	*65*	*54*	*53*	*57*	*61*	*54*	*80*	*55*	*57*	*59*

Key: Coun.=Council; F=Female; M=Male; Priv.=Private; Stud.=Student.

TABLE 5.8

Respondent is . . . .
Base: All respondents

Figures in bold italic are percentages

	Total	Sex		Age			Class		No. in household			Respondent		Police		Tenure			Victim	
		M	F	16–34	35–54	55+	ABC1	C2DE	1	2	3+	Works	Stud.	Good	Not good	Own/ buying	Coun.	Priv.	Yes	No
Total	259	108	151	87	62	107	139	119	67	89	103	102	38	166	93	155	44	47	76	183
Working full-time	68	44	24	23	35	9	34	34	11	17	40	68	–	49	19	52	7	6	26	42
	26	*41*	*16*	*26*	*56*	*8*	*24*	*29*	*16*	*19*	*39*	*67*	–	*30*	*20*	*34*	*16*	*13*	*34*	*23*
Working part-time	34	3	31	11	16	5	12	22	6	9	19	34	–	20	14	20	10	1	10	24
	13	*3*	*21*	*13*	*26*	*5*	*9*	*18*	*9*	*10*	*18*	*33*	–	*12*	*15*	*13*	*23*	*2*	*13*	*13*
Waiting to start an obtained job	2	1	1	1	1	–	2	–	1	–	1	–	–	2	–	–	1	1	–	2
	1	*1*	*1*	*1*	*2*	–	*1*	–	*1*	–	*1*	–	–	*1*	–	–	*2*	*2*	–	*1*
Looking for work	4	3	1	3	1	–	1	3	1	1	2	–	–	2	2	2	1	1	1	3
	2	*3*	*1*	*3*	*2*	–	*1*	*3*	*1*	*1*	*2*	–	–	*1*	*2*	*1*	*2*	*2*	*1*	*2*
Temporarily sick	–	–	–	–	–	–	–	–	–	–	–	–	–	–	–	–	–	–	–	–
	–	–	–	–	–	–	–	–	–	–	–	–	–	–	–	–	–	–	–	–
Full-time student	38	18	20	37	1	–	37	1	23	2	13	–	38	26	12	3	2	32	18	20
	15	*17*	*13*	*43*	*2*	–	*27*	*1*	*34*	*2*	*13*	–	*100*	*16*	*13*	*2*	*5*	*68*	*24*	*11*
Long-time sick	3	2	1	–	–	3	1	2	–	2	1	–	–	1	2	2	–	1	–	3
	1	*2*	*1*	–	–	*3*	*1*	*2*	–	*2*	*1*	–	–	*1*	*2*	*1*	–	*2*	–	*2*
Wholly retired	72	36	36	–	1	71	35	37	22	42	8	–	–	43	29	56	10	3	9	63
	28	*33*	*24*	–	*2*	*66*	*25*	*31*	*33*	*47*	*8*	–	–	*26*	*31*	*36*	*23*	*6*	*12*	*34*
Keeping house	32	–	32	9	6	17	14	17	2	13	17	–	–	18	14	18	11	1	8	24
	12	–	*21*	*10*	*10*	*16*	*10*	*14*	*3*	*15*	*17*	–	–	*11*	*15*	*12*	*25*	*2*	*11*	*13*
Something else	5	1	4	2	1	2	2	3	1	3	1	–	–	4	1	1	2	1	3	2
	2	*1*	*3*	*2*	*2*	*2*	*1*	*3*	*1*	*3*	*1*	–	–	*2*	*1*	*1*	*5*	*2*	*4*	*1*
No response	1	–	1	1	–	–	1	–	–	–	1	–	–	1	–	1	–	–	1	–
	*	–	*1*	*1*	–	–	*1*	–	–	–	*1*	–	–	*1*	–	*1*	–	–	*1*	–

Key: Coun.=Council; F=Female; M=Male; Priv.=Private; Stud.=Student.
* less than 0.5.

TABLE 5.9

Respondent is aged . . .
Base: All respondents

Figures in bold italic are percentages

	Total	Sex		Age			Class		No. in household			Respondent		Police		Tenure			Victim	
		M	F	16–34	35–54	55+	ABC1	C2DE	1	2	3+	Works	Stud.	Good	Not good	Own/buying	Coun.	Priv.	Yes	No
Total	259	108	151	87	62	107	139	119	67	89	103	102	38	166	93	155	44	47	76	183
16–24	50	23	27	50	-	-	38	12	25	1	24	11	31	36	14	9	6	33	24	26
	19	*21*	*18*	*57*	-	-	*27*	*10*	*37*	*1*	*23*	*11*	*82*	*22*	*15*	*6*	*14*	*70*	*32*	*14*
25–34	37	12	25	37	-	-	15	22	7	10	20	23	6	24	13	19	9	8	14	23
	14	*11*	*17*	*43*	-	-	*11*	*18*	*10*	*11*	*19*	*23*	*16*	*14*	*14*	*12*	*20*	*17*	*18*	*13*
35–54	62	24	38	-	62	-	33	29	8	12	42	51	1	44	18	44	13	2	18	44
	24	*22*	*25*	-	*100*	-	*24*	*24*	*12*	*13*	*41*	*50*	*3*	*27*	*19*	*28*	*30*	*4*	*24*	*24*
55+	107	48	59	-	-	107	52	54	25	66	16	14	-	59	48	81	16	4	18	89
	41	*44*	*39*	-	-	*100*	*37*	*45*	*37*	*74*	*16*	*14*	-	*36*	*52*	*52*	*36*	*9*	*24*	*49*
No response	3	1	2	-	-	-	1	2	2	-	1	3	-	3	-	2	-	-	2	1
	1	*1*	*1*	-	-	-	*1*	*2*	*3*	-	*1*	*3*	-	*2*	-	*1*	-	-	*3*	*1*

Key: Coun.=Council; F=Female; M=Male; Priv.=Private; Stud.=Student.

TABLE 5.10

Social class
Base: All respondents

Figures in bold italic are percentages

	Total	Sex		Age			Class		No. in household			Respondent		Police		Tenure			Victim	
		M	F	16–34	35–54	55+	ABC1	C2DE	1	2	3+	Works	Stud.	Good	Not good	Own/buying	Coun.	Priv.	Yes	No
Total	259	108	151	87	62	107	139	119	67	89	103	102	38	166	93	155	44	47	76	183
AB	45	22	23	4	16	25	45	-	9	22	14	21	-	26	19	41	-	3	12	33
	17	*20*	*15*	*5*	*26*	*23*	*32*	*-*	*13*	*25*	*14*	*21*	*-*	*16*	*20*	*26*	*-*	*6*	*16*	*18*
C1	94	36	58	49	17	27	94	-	36	21	37	25	37	61	33	48	6	37	30	64
	36	*33*	*38*	*56*	*27*	*25*	*68*	*-*	*54*	*24*	*36*	*25*	*97*	*37*	*35*	*31*	*14*	*79*	*39*	*35*
C2	47	22	25	17	16	13	-	47	4	13	30	31	-	37	10	30	13	1	14	33
	18	*20*	*17*	*20*	*26*	*12*	*-*	*39*	*6*	*15*	*29*	*30*	*-*	*22*	*11*	*19*	*30*	*2*	*18*	*18*
DE	72	28	44	17	13	41	-	72	18	32	22	25	1	41	31	35	25	6	20	52
	28	*26*	*29*	*20*	*21*	*38*	*-*	*61*	*27*	*36*	*21*	*25*	*3*	*25*	*33*	*23*	*57*	*13*	*26*	*28*
No response	1	-	1	-	-	1	-	-	-	1	-	-	-	1	-	1	-	-	-	1
	***	*-*	*1*	*-*	*-*	*1*	*-*	*-*	*-*	*1*	*-*	*-*	*-*	*1*	*-*	*1*	*-*	*-*	*-*	*1*

Key: Coun.=Council; F=Female; M=Male; Priv.=Private; Stud.=Student.
*=less than .5

TABLE 5.11

Total number of incidents
Base: All respondents

Figures in bold italic are percentages

	Total	Sex		Age			Class		No. in household			Respondent		Police		Tenure			Victim	
		M	F	16–34	35–54	55+	ABC1	C2DE	1	2	3+	Works	Stud.	Good	Not good	Own/ buying	Coun.	Priv.	Yes	No
Total	259	108	151	87	62	107	139	119	67	89	103	102	38	166	93	155	44	47	76	183
None	183	75	108	49	44	89	97	85	46	69	68	66	20	117	66	106	38	30	-	183
	71	*69*	*72*	*56*	*71*	*83*	*70*	*71*	*69*	*78*	*66*	*65*	*53*	*70*	*71*	*68*	*86*	*64*	*-*	*100*
1	41	18	23	20	11	9	20	21	10	13	18	22	9	25	16	27	2	9	41	-
	16	*17*	*15*	*23*	*18*	*8*	*14*	*18*	*15*	*15*	*17*	*22*	*24*	*15*	*17*	*17*	*5*	*19*	*54*	*-*
2	17	7	10	8	2	6	10	7	5	4	8	7	4	11	6	11	2	4	17	-
	7	*6*	*7*	*9*	*3*	*6*	*7*	*6*	*7*	*4*	*8*	*7*	*11*	*7*	*6*	*7*	*5*	*9*	*22*	*-*
3	5	3	2	3	-	2	3	2	1	2	2	2	2	4	1	3	-	1	5	-
	2	*3*	*1*	*3*	*-*	*2*	*2*	*2*	*1*	*2*	*2*	*2*	*5*	*2*	*1*	*2*	*-*	*2*	*7*	*-*
4	4	1	3	3	1	-	4	-	2	-	2	1	2	3	1	2	-	2	4	-
	2	*1*	*2*	*3*	*2*	*-*	*3*	*-*	*3*	*-*	*2*	*1*	*5*	*2*	*1*	*1*	*-*	*4*	*5*	*-*
5+	9	4	5	4	4	1	5	4	3	1	5	4	1	6	3	6	2	1	9	-
	3	*4*	*3*	*5*	*6*	*1*	*4*	*3*	*4*	*1*	*5*	*4*	*3*	*4*	*3*	*4*	*5*	*2*	*12*	*-*
Mean score	0.73	0.74	0.73	1.20	0.74	0.35	0.86	0.60	0.93	0.36	0.93	0.71	1.16	0.78	0.65	0.80	0.43	0.87	2.50	0.00

Key: Coun.=Council; F=Female; M=Male; Priv.=Private; Stud.=Student.

TABLE 5.12

Screening question at which this incident or series of similar incidents was mentioned
Base: All victims

Figures in bold italic are percentages

	Total	Sex		Age			Class		No. in household			Respondent		Police		Tenure			Victim
		M	F	16-34	35-54	55+	ABC1	C2DE	1	2	3+	Works	Stud.	Good	Not good	Own/buying	Coun.	Priv.	Yes
Total	116	50	66	63	28	23	73	43	35	29	52	53	31	77	39	74	7	29	116
Vehicle theft	1	-	1	-	1	-	-	1	-	-	1	-	-	1	-	1	-	-	1
Vehicle theft %	*1*	*-*	*2*	*-*	*4*	*-*	*-*	*2*	*-*	*-*	*2*	*-*	*-*	*1*	*-*	*1*	*-*	*-*	*1*
Theft from vehicle	12	3	9	5	4	3	7	5	2	4	6	5	2	8	4	10	1	1	12
Theft from vehicle %	*10*	*6*	*14*	*8*	*14*	*13*	*10*	*12*	*6*	*14*	*12*	*9*	*6*	*10*	*10*	*14*	*14*	*3*	*10*
Vehicle damage	30	16	14	14	7	8	16	14	4	10	16	17	5	19	11	22	1	5	30
Vehicle damage %	*26*	*32*	*21*	*22*	*25*	*35*	*22*	*33*	*11*	*34*	*31*	*32*	*16*	*25*	*28*	*30*	*14*	*17*	*26*
Bicycle theft	1	-	1	-	1	-	-	1	-	1	-	-	-	-	1	-	-	-	1
Bicycle theft %	*1*	*-*	*2*	*-*	*4*	*-*	*-*	*2*	*-*	*3*	*-*	*-*	*-*	*-*	*3*	*-*	*-*	*-*	*1*
Burglary (movers)	2	-	2	2	-	-	2	-	1	-	1	-	2	1	1	-	-	2	2
Burglary (movers) %	*2*	*-*	*3*	*3*	*-*	*-*	*3*	*-*	*3*	*-*	*2*	*-*	*6*	*1*	*3*	*-*	*-*	*7*	*2*
Break-in with damage (movers)	2	-	2	2	-	-	1	1	1	-	1	-	1	1	1	-	1	1	2
Break-in with damage (movers) %	*2*	*-*	*3*	*3*	*-*	*-*	*1*	*2*	*3*	*-*	*2*	*-*	*3*	*1*	*3*	*-*	*14*	*3*	*2*
Attempted burglary (movers)	1	-	1	1	-	-	1	-	1	-	-	-	1	1	-	-	-	1	1
Attempted burglary (movers) %	*1*	*-*	*2*	*2*	*-*	*-*	*1*	*-*	*3*	*-*	*-*	*-*	*3*	*1*	*-*	*-*	*-*	*3*	*1*
Theft from dwelling (movers)	1	1	-	-	1	1	-	1	1	-	-	-	-	-	1	-	-	-	1
Theft from dwelling (movers) %	*1*	*2*	*-*	*-*	*4*	*4*	*-*	*2*	*3*	*-*	*-*	*-*	*-*	*-*	*3*	*1*	*-*	*-*	*1*
Theft outside building (movers)	1	-	1	1	-	-	1	-	1	-	-	-	1	1	-	-	-	1	1
Theft outside building (movers) %	*1*	*-*	*2*	*2*	*-*	*-*	*1*	*-*	*3*	*-*	*-*	*-*	*3*	*1*	*-*	*-*	*-*	*3*	*1*
Vandalism (movers)	2	1	1	2	-	-	2	-	2	-	-	-	2	2	-	-	-	2	2
Vandalism (movers) %	*2*	*2*	*2*	*3*	*-*	*-*	*3*	*-*	*6*	*-*	*-*	*-*	*6*	*3*	*-*	*-*	*-*	*7*	*2*
Burglary	3	1	2	1	1	1	3	-	2	1	-	1	1	3	-	2	-	1	3
Burglary %	*3*	*2*	*3*	*2*	*4*	*4*	*4*	*-*	*6*	*3*	*-*	*2*	*3*	*4*	*-*	*3*	*-*	*3*	*3*
Break-in with damage	1	-	1	1	-	-	-	1	-	1	-	1	-	1	-	1	-	-	1
Break-in with damage %	*1*	*-*	*2*	*2*	*-*	*-*	*-*	*2*	*-*	*3*	*-*	*2*	*-*	*1*	*-*	*1*	*-*	*-*	*1*

Key: Coun.=Council; F=Female; M=Male; Priv.=Private; Stud.=Student.

TABLE 5.12 (continued)

Screening question at which this incident or series of similar incidents was mentioned
Base: All victims

Figures in bold italic are percentages

	Total	Sex		Age			Class		No. in household			Respondent		Police		Tenure			Victim
		M	F	16–34	35–54	55+	ABC1	C2DE	1	2	3+	Works	Stud.	Good	Not good	Own/buying	Coun.	Priv.	Yes
Total	116	50	66	63	28	23	73	43	35	29	52	53	31	77	39	74	7	29	116
Attempted burglary	7	3	4	2	2	2	4	3	3	2	2	4	1	4	3	5	1	1	7
	6	***6***	***6***	***3***	***7***	***9***	***5***	***7***	***9***	***7***	***4***	***8***	***3***	***5***	***8***	***7***	***14***	***3***	***6***
Theft from dwelling	2	1	1	1	-	1	1	1	1	1	-	1	1	2	-	1	-	1	2
	2	***2***	***2***	***2***	-	***4***	***1***	***2***	***3***	***3***	-	***2***	***3***	***3***	-	***1***	-	***3***	***2***
Theft from outside dwelling (not milk bot.)	12	4	8	5	3	4	9	3	1	4	7	7	-	5	7	11	1	-	12
	10	***8***	***12***	***8***	***11***	***17***	***12***	***7***	***3***	***14***	***13***	***13***	-	***6***	***18***	***15***	***14***	-	***10***
Vandalism	3	1	2	3	-	-	1	2	1	-	2	1	1	3	-	1	1	1	3
	3	***2***	***3***	***5***	-	-	***1***	***5***	***3***	-	***4***	***2***	***3***	***4***	-	***1***	***14***	***3***	***3***
Theft from person	-	-	-	-	-	-	-	-	-	-	-	-	-	-	-	-	-	-	-
	-	-	-	-	-	-	-	-	-	-	-	-	-	-	-	-	-	-	-
Attempted theft from person	1	-	1	1	-	-	1	-	1	-	-	-	1	1	-	1	-	1	1
	1	-	***2***	***2***	-	-	***1***	-	***3***	-	-	-	***3***	***1***	-	***1***	-	***1***	***1***
Other theft	12	8	4	5	5	2	6	6	4	3	5	6	4	7	5	7	1	4	12
	10	***16***	***6***	***8***	***18***	***9***	***8***	***14***	***11***	***10***	***10***	***11***	***13***	***9***	***13***	***9***	***14***	***14***	***10***
Damage to property	3	2	1	2	-	1	3	-	2	1	-	2	1	2	1	2	-	1	3
	3	***4***	***2***	***3***	-	***4***	***4***	-	***6***	***3***	-	***4***	***3***	***3***	***3***	***3***	-	***3***	***3***
Assault	11	6	5	9	2	-	7	4	2	1	8	6	2	8	3	7	2	2	11
	9	***12***	***8***	***14***	***7***	-	***10***	***9***	***6***	***3***	***15***	***11***	***6***	***10***	***8***	***9***	***7***	***11***	***9***
Threats	7	3	4	5	2	-	7	-	4	-	3	2	4	6	1	3	3	3	7
	6	***6***	***6***	***8***	***7***	-	***10***	-	***11***	-	***6***	***4***	***13***	***8***	***3***	***4***	***10***	***6***	***6***
Sexual assault	1	-	1	1	-	-	1	-	1	-	-	-	1	1	-	-	-	1	1
	1	-	***2***	***2***	-	-	***1***	-	***3***	-	-	-	***3***	***1***	-	-	-	***3***	***1***

Key: Coun.=Council; F=Female; M=Male; Priv.=Private; Stud.=Student.

TABLE 5.13

Q. Why did you not notify the police?
Base: All where the police did not come to know about the crime

Figures in bold italic are percentages

	Total	Sex		Age			Class		No. in household			Respondent		Police		Tenure			Victim
		M	F	16–34	35–54	55+	ABC1	C2DE	1	2	3+	Works	Stud.	Good	Not good	Own/buying	Coun.	Priv.	Yes
Total	64	34	30	38	15	11	42	22	17	16	31	27	19	42	22	40	4	18	64
Private/personal/family matter	3 / ***5***	- / -	3 / ***10***	3 / ***8***	-	-	1 / ***2***	2 / ***9***	1 / ***6***	-	2 / ***6***	1 / ***4***	1 / ***5***	3 / ***7***	-	1 / ***3***	-	1 / ***6***	3 / ***5***
Dealt with matter myself/ourselves	4 / ***6***	3 / ***9***	1 / ***3***	3 / ***8***	-	1 / ***9***	2 / ***5***	2 / ***9***	2 / ***12***	-	2 / ***6***	2 / ***7***	1 / ***5***	3 / ***7***	1 / ***5***	2 / ***5***	-	2 / ***11***	4 / ***6***
Reported to other authorities (e.g superiors, company security staff, etc.)	- / -	-	-	-	-	-	-	-	-	-	-	-	-	-	-	-	-	-	-
Dislike/fear of police	3 / ***5***	3 / ***9***	-	3 / ***8***	-	-	3 / ***7***	-	-	-	3 / ***10***	3 / ***11***	-	-	3 / ***14***	3 / ***8***	-	-	3 / ***5***
Fear of reprisal by offenders/make matters worse	2 / ***3***	2 / ***6***	-	1 / ***3***	1 / ***7***	-	2 / ***5***	-	-	1 / ***6***	1 / ***3***	1 / ***4***	-	2 / ***5***	-	2 / ***5***	-	-	2 / ***3***
Police could have done nothing	8 / ***13***	5 / ***15***	3 / ***10***	6 / ***16***	-	2 / ***18***	3 / ***7***	5 / ***23***	-	4 / ***25***	4 / ***13***	4 / ***15***	1 / ***5***	6 / ***14***	2 / ***9***	5 / ***13***	1 / ***25***	2 / ***11***	8 / ***13***
Police would not have bothered/not been interested	3 / ***5***	2 / ***6***	1 / ***3***	2 / ***5***	-	1 / ***9***	1 / ***2***	2 / ***9***	-	1 / ***6***	2 / ***6***	2 / ***7***	-	1 / ***2***	2 / ***9***	3 / ***8***	-	-	3 / ***5***
Inconvenient/too much trouble	- / -	-	-	-	-	-	-	-	-	-	-	-	-	-	-	-	-	-	-
No loss/damage/attempt at offence was unsuccessful	1 / ***2***	-	1 / ***3***	1 / ***3***	-	-	1 / ***2***	-	1 / ***6***	-	-	-	1 / ***5***	1 / ***2***	-	-	-	1 / ***6***	1 / ***2***

Key: Coun.=Council; F=Female; M=Male; Priv.=Private; Stud.=Student.

TABLE 5.13 (continued)

Q. Why did you not notify the police?
Base: All where the police did not come to know about the crime

Figures in bold italic are percentages

	Total	Sex		Age			Class		No. in household			Respondent		Police		Tenure			Victim
		M	F	16–34	35–54	55+	ABC1	C2DE	1	2	3+	Works	Stud.	Good	Not good	Own/ buying	Coun.	Priv.	Yes
Total	64	34	30	38	15	11	42	22	17	16	31	27	19	42	22	40	4	18	64
Too trivial/not worth	33	17	16	16	10	7	24	9	11	7	15	11	13	20	13	21	2	10	33
reporting	*52*	*50*	*53*	*42*	*67*	*64*	*57*	*41*	*65*	*44*	*48*	*41*	*68*	*48*	*59*	*53*	*50*	*56*	*52*
Other	9	3	6	5	4	-	8	1	3	2	4	4	3	7	2	4	1	3	9
	14	*9*	*20*	*13*	*27*	-	*19*	*5*	*18*	*13*	*13*	*15*	*16*	*17*	*9*	*10*	*25*	*17*	*14*
No response	1	1	-	1	-	-	1	1	-	1	-	1	-	-	1	1	-	-	1
	2	*3*	*3*	*3*	-	-	*5*	*5*	-	*6*	-	*4*	-	-	*5*	*3*	-	-	*2*

Key: Coun.=Council; F=Female; M=Male; Priv.=Private; Stud.=Student.

TABLE 5.14

Q. How much interest did the police show in what you/he/she had to say?
Base: All where the police did come to know about the crime

Figures in bold italic are percentages

	Total	Sex		Age			Class		No. in household			Respondent		Police		Tenure			Victim
		M	F	16–34	35–54	55+	ABC1	C2DE	1	2	3+	Works	Stud.	Good	Not good	Own/ buying	Coun.	Priv.	Yes
Total	52	16	36	25	13	12	31	21	18	13	21	26	12	35	17	34	3	11	52
As much as you thought they should	35 / *67*	8 / *50*	27 / *75*	13 / *52*	11 / *85*	9 / *75*	23 / *74*	12 / *57*	14 / *78*	8 / *62*	13 / *62*	16 / *62*	9 / *75*	25 / *71*	10 / *59*	21 / *62*	3 / *100*	7 / *64*	35 / *67*
Less than you thought they should	12 / *23*	6 / *38*	6 / *17*	8 / *32*	1 / *8*	3 / *25*	5 / *16*	7 / *33*	2 / *11*	5 / *38*	5 / *24*	8 / *31*	1 / *8*	7 / *20*	5 / *29*	10 / *29*	– / –	2 / *18*	12 / *23*
Don't know	3 / *6*	2 / *13*	1 / *3*	3 / *12*	– / –	– / –	2 / *6*	1 / *5*	2 / *11*	– / –	1 / *5*	1 / *4*	2 / *17*	2 / *6*	1 / *6*	1 / *3*	– / –	2 / *18*	3 / *6*
No response	2 / *4*	– / –	2 / *6*	1 / *4*	1 / *8*	– / –	1 / *3*	1 / *5*	– / –	– / –	2 / *10*	1 / *4*	– / –	1 / *3*	1 / *6*	2 / *6*	– / –	– / –	2 / *4*

Key: Coun.=Council; F=Female; M=Male; Priv.=Private; Stud.=Student.

TABLE 5.15

Q. Overall, were you/(the victim) satisfied or dissatisfied with the way the police handled this matter?
Base: All where the police did come to know about the crime

Figures in bold italic are percentages

	Total	Sex		Age			Class		No. in household			Respondent		Police		Tenure			Victim
		M	F	16–34	35–54	55+	ABC1	C2DE	1	2	3+	Works	Stud.	Good	Not good	Own/ buying	Coun.	Priv.	Yes
Total	52	16	36	25	13	12	31	21	18	13	21	26	12	35	17	34	3	11	52
Very satisfied (2)	18	3	15	5	6	6	13	5	8	4	6	9	4	11	7	12	2	2	18
(bold italic)	*35*	*19*	*42*	*20*	*46*	*50*	*42*	*24*	*44*	*31*	*29*	*35*	*33*	*31*	*41*	*35*	*67*	*18*	*35*
Fairly satisfied (1)	16	6	10	7	5	3	7	9	6	2	8	7	4	11	5	9	1	4	16
(bold italic)	*31*	*38*	*28*	*28*	*38*	*25*	*23*	*43*	*33*	*15*	*38*	*27*	*33*	*31*	*29*	*26*	*33*	*36*	*31*
A bit dissatisfied (-1)	8	4	4	4	1	3	6	2	2	4	2	4	2	6	2	6	-	2	8
(bold italic)	*15*	*25*	*11*	*16*	*8*	*25*	*19*	*10*	*11*	*31*	*10*	*15*	*17*	*17*	*12*	*18*	*-*	*18*	*15*
Very dissatisfied (-2)	5	2	3	5	-	-	1	4	1	3	1	4	1	3	2	3	-	2	5
(bold italic)	*10*	*13*	*8*	*20*	*-*	*-*	*3*	*19*	*6*	*23*	*5*	*15*	*8*	*9*	*12*	*9*	*-*	*18*	*10*
Too early to say	-	-	-	-	-	-	-	-	-	-	-	-	-	-	-	-	-	-	-
(bold italic)	*-*	*-*	*-*	*-*	*-*	*-*	*-*	*-*	*-*	*-*	*-*	*-*	*-*	*-*	*-*	*-*	*-*	*-*	*-*
Don't know	3	1	2	3	-	-	3	-	1	-	2	1	1	3	-	2	-	1	3
(bold italic)	*6*	*6*	*6*	*12*	*-*	*-*	*10*	*-*	*6*	*-*	*10*	*4*	*8*	*9*	*-*	*6*	*-*	*9*	*6*
No response	2	-	2	1	1	-	1	1	-	-	2	1	-	1	1	2	-	-	2
(bold italic)	*4*	*-*	*6*	*4*	*8*	*-*	*3*	*5*	*-*	*-*	*10*	*4*	*-*	*3*	*6*	*6*	*-*	*-*	*4*

Key: Coun.=Council; F=Female; M=Male; Priv.=Private; Stud.=Student.

TABLE 5.16

Q. I would now like to ask you how serious a crime you personally think this was. How would you rate this crime on the scale from 0 to 20?

Base: All victims

Figures in bold italic are percentages

	Total	Sex		Age			Class		No. in household			Respondent		Police		Tenure			Victim
		M	F	16–34	35–54	55+	ABC1	C2DE	1	2	3+	Works	Stud.	Good	Not good	Own/ buying	Coun.	Priv.	Yes
Total	116	50	66	63	28	23	73	43	35	29	52	53	31	77	39	74	7	29	116
None	10	6	4	4	5	1	7	3	5	1	4	6	4	9	1	6	1	3	10
	9	*12*	*6*	*6*	*18*	*4*	*10*	*7*	*14*	*3*	*8*	*11*	*13*	*12*	*3*	*8*	*14*	*10*	*9*
1	15	8	7	10	3	2	9	6	6	3	6	6	6	11	4	8	1	6	15
	13	*16*	*11*	*16*	*11*	*9*	*12*	*14*	*17*	*10*	*12*	*11*	*19*	*14*	*10*	*11*	*14*	*21*	*13*
2	11	1	10	7	-	4	8	3	2	6	3	3	4	6	5	7	1	2	11
	9	*2*	*15*	*11*	-	*17*	*11*	*7*	*6*	*21*	*6*	*6*	*13*	*8*	*13*	*9*	*14*	*7*	*9*
3	9	5	4	7	1	1	5	4	2	3	4	5	3	5	4	7	-	2	9
	8	*10*	*6*	*11*	*4*	*4*	*7*	*9*	*6*	*10*	*8*	*9*	*10*	*6*	*10*	*9*	-	*7*	*8*
4	8	5	3	5	-	3	2	6	3	2	3	5	1	2	6	4	2	2	8
	7	*10*	*5*	*8*	-	*13*	*3*	*14*	*9*	*7*	*6*	*9*	*3*	*3*	*15*	*5*	*29*	*7*	*7*
5	20	9	11	11	5	3	12	8	5	2	13	9	4	13	7	15	1	4	20
	17	*18*	*17*	*17*	*18*	*13*	*16*	*19*	*14*	*7*	*25*	*17*	*13*	*17*	*18*	*20*	*14*	*14*	*17*
6	7	2	5	4	2	1	4	3	2	2	3	3	2	5	2	3	-	3	7
	6	*4*	*8*	*6*	*7*	*4*	*5*	*7*	*6*	*7*	*6*	*6*	*6*	*6*	*5*	*4*	-	*10*	*6*
7	6	1	5	3	2	1	6	-	1	2	3	2	2	5	1	4	-	1	6
	5	*2*	*8*	*5*	*7*	*4*	*8*	-	*3*	*7*	*6*	*4*	*6*	*6*	*3*	*5*	-	*3*	*5*
8	3	3	-	-	-	3	1	2	3	-	-	-	-	2	1	1	-	1	3
	3	*6*	-	-	-	*13*	*1*	*5*	*9*	-	-	-	-	*3*	*3*	*1*	-	*3*	*3*
9	-	-	-	-	-	-	-	-	-	-	-	-	-	-	-	-	-	-	-
	-	-	-	-	-	-	-	-	-	-	-	-	-	-	-	-	-	-	-
10	8	3	5	4	2	2	6	2	1	3	4	6	1	6	2	6	1	1	8
	7	*6*	*8*	*6*	*7*	*9*	*8*	*5*	*3*	*10*	*8*	*11*	*3*	*8*	*5*	*8*	-	*3*	*7*
11	1	-	1	1	-	-	1	-	-	-	1	1	1	1	-	-	-	-	1
	1	-	*2*	*2*	-	-	*1*	-	-	-	*2*	-	*3*	*1*	-	-	-	-	*1*

TABLE 5.16 (continued)

Q. I would now like to ask you how serious a crime you personally think this was. How would you rate this crime on the scale from 0 to 20?

Base: All victims

Figures in bold italic are percentages

	Total	Sex		Age			Class		No. in household			Respondent		Police		Tenure			Victim
		M	F	16-34	35-54	55+	ABC1	C2DE	1	2	3+	Works	Stud.	Good	Not good	Own/ buying	Coun.	Priv.	Yes
Total	116	50	66	63	28	23	73	43	35	29	52	53	31	77	39	74	7	29	116
12	5	2	3	3	1	1	4	1	2	1	2	-	2	4	1	3	1	2	5
	4	***4***	***5***	***5***	***4***	***4***	***5***	***2***	***6***	***3***	***4***	***-***	***6***	***5***	***3***	***4***	***-***	***7***	***4***
13	1	1	-	1	-	-	1	-	-	-	1	1	-	-	1	1	-	-	1
	1	***2***	***-***	***2***	***-***	***-***	***1***	***-***	***-***	***-***	***2***	***2***	***-***	***-***	***3***	***1***	***-***	***-***	***1***
14	2	2	-	-	1	1	1	1	-	2	-	1	-	2	-	2	-	-	2
	2	***4***	***-***	***-***	***4***	***4***	***1***	***2***	***-***	***7***	***-***	***2***	***-***	***3***	***-***	***3***	***-***	***-***	***2***
15	5	2	3	2	3	-	3	2	-	2	3	4	-	2	3	3	1	1	5
	4	***4***	***5***	***3***	***11***	***-***	***4***	***5***	***-***	***7***	***6***	***8***	***-***	***3***	***8***	***4***	***14***	***3***	***4***
16	1	1	1	1	-	-	-	1	1	-	-	1	-	1	-	1	-	-	1
	1	***-***	***2***	***-***	***-***	***-***	***-***	***2***	***3***	***-***	***-***	***2***	***-***	***1***	***-***	***1***	***-***	***-***	***1***
17	1	-	1	-	1	-	-	1	-	-	1	-	-	1	-	1	-	-	1
	1	***-***	***2***	***-***	***4***	***-***	***-***	***2***	***-***	***-***	***2***	***-***	***-***	***1***	***-***	***1***	***-***	***-***	***1***
18	1	1	1	1	-	-	1	-	1	-	-	-	1	1	-	-	-	1	1
	1	***1***	***2***	***2***	***-***	***-***	***1***	***-***	***3***	***-***	***-***	***-***	***3***	***1***	***-***	***-***	***-***	***3***	***1***
19	2	-	2	-	2	-	2	-	1	-	1	1	-	1	1	2	-	-	2
	2	***-***	***3***	***-***	***7***	***-***	***3***	***-***	***3***	***-***	***2***	***2***	***-***	***1***	***3***	***3***	***-***	***-***	***2***
20	-	-	-	-	-	-	-	-	-	-	-	-	-	-	-	-	-	-	-
Don't know	-	-	-	-	-	-	-	-	-	-	-	-	-	-	-	-	-	-	-
Mean Score	5.69	5.16	6.09	4.97	7.25	5.35	5.88	5.37	5.23	5.79	5.94	5.77	4.39	5.70	5.67	5.96	4.43	4.97	5.69

Key: Coun.=Council; F=Female; M=Male; Priv.=Private; Stud.=Student.

TABLE 5.17

Q. Which of these do you think should have happened to the person/people who comitted the crime(s)?
Base: All victims

Figures in bold italic are percentages

	Total	Sex		Age			Class		No. in household			Respondent		Police		Tenure			Victim
		M	F	16–34	35–54	55+	ABC1	C2DE	1	2	3+	Works	Stud.	Good	Not good	Own/buying	Coun.	Priv.	Yes
Total	116	50	66	63	28	23	73	43	35	29	52	53	31	77	39	74	7	29	116
Nothing/not a matter for the police	14	8	6	11	2	1	10	4	3	1	10	6	5	11	3	8	1	4	14
(%)	*12*	*16*	*9*	*17*	*7*	*4*	*14*	*9*	*9*	*3*	*19*	*11*	*16*	*14*	*8*	*11*	*14*	*14*	*12*
Get an informal warning from the police	16	5	11	7	5	3	12	4	4	3	9	8	4	9	7	10	2	3	16
(%)	*14*	*10*	*17*	*11*	*18*	*13*	*16*	*9*	*11*	*10*	*17*	*15*	*13*	*12*	*18*	*14*	*29*	*10*	*14*
Get a formal caution from the police	12	6	6	8	3	1	6	6	6	–	6	5	4	10	2	6	1	5	12
(%)	*10*	*12*	*9*	*13*	*11*	*4*	*8*	*14*	*17*	*–*	*12*	*9*	*13*	*13*	*5*	*8*	*14*	*17*	*10*
Go to court but only get a warning	5	3	2	5	–	–	5	–	2	–	3	1	3	4	1	2	–	2	5
(%)	*4*	*6*	*3*	*8*	*–*	*–*	*7*	*–*	*6*	*–*	*6*	*2*	*10*	*5*	*3*	*3*	*–*	*7*	*4*
Have to pay compensation	31	10	21	17	8	5	16	15	6	12	13	23	5	19	12	25	–	5	31
(%)	*27*	*20*	*32*	*27*	*29*	*22*	*22*	*35*	*17*	*41*	*25*	*43*	*16*	*25*	*31*	*34*	*–*	*17*	*27*
Get a suspended prison sentence	1	1	–	1	–	–	1	–	1	–	–	–	1	1	–	–	–	1	1
(%)	*1*	*2*	*–*	*2*	*–*	*–*	*1*	*–*	*3*	*–*	*–*	*–*	*3*	*1*	*–*	*–*	*–*	*3*	*1*
Have to do community service	8	4	4	2	2	4	6	2	2	3	3	–	2	5	3	6	–	2	8
(%)	*7*	*8*	*6*	*3*	*7*	*17*	*8*	*5*	*6*	*10*	*6*	*–*	*6*	*6*	*8*	*8*	*–*	*7*	*7*
Be put on probation	3	–	3	–	1	2	–	3	2	–	1	–	–	1	2	1	2	–	3
(%)	*3*	*–*	*5*	*–*	*4*	*9*	*–*	*7*	*6*	*–*	*2*	*–*	*–*	*1*	*5*	*1*	*29*	*–*	*3*
Be fined under £50	3	2	1	2	–	1	3	–	1	1	1	1	1	2	1	2	–	1	3
(%)	*3*	*4*	*2*	*3*	*–*	*4*	*4*	*–*	*3*	*3*	*2*	*2*	*3*	*3*	*3*	*3*	*–*	*3*	*3*
Be fined £50 or more	4	3	1	2	–	2	1	3	–	2	2	1	1	2	2	4	–	–	4
(%)	*3*	*6*	*2*	*3*	*–*	*9*	*1*	*7*	*–*	*7*	*5*	*2*	*3*	*3*	*5*	*5*	*–*	*–*	*3*
Go to prison or similar for under a year	3	3	–	1	1	1	2	1	1	1	1	2	–	1	2	3	–	–	3
(%)	*3*	*6*	*–*	*2*	*4*	*4*	*3*	*2*	*3*	*3*	*2*	*4*	*–*	*1*	*5*	*4*	*–*	*–*	*3*
Go to prison or similar for 1 to 5 years	4	1	3	2	2	–	3	1	2	2	–	3	1	3	1	2	–	2	4
(%)	*3*	*2*	*5*	*3*	*7*	*–*	*4*	*2*	*6*	*7*	*–*	*6*	*3*	*4*	*3*	*3*	*–*	*7*	*3*

TABLE 5.17 (continued)

Q. Which of these do you think should have happened to the person/people who comitted the crime(s)?
Base: All victims

Figures in bold italic are percentages

	Total	Sex		Age			Class		No. in household			Respondent		Police		Tenure			Victim
		M	F	16–34	35–54	55+	ABC1	C2DE	1	2	3+	Works	Stud.	Good	Not good	Own/ buying	Coun.	Priv.	Yes
Total	116	50	66	63	28	23	73	43	35	29	52	53	31	77	39	74	7	29	116
Go to prison or similar	2	-	2	2	-	-	2	-	-	-	-	-	2	2	-	-	-	2	2
for over 5 years	***2***	***-***	***3***	***3***	***-***	***-***	***3***	***-***	***6***	***-***	***-***	***-***	***6***	***3***	***-***	***-***	***-***	***7***	***2***
Other	3	2	1	-	2	1	2	1	1	2	-	2	-	3	-	3	-	-	3
	3	***4***	***2***	***-***	***7***	***4***	***3***	***2***	***3***	***7***	***-***	***4***	***-***	***4***	***-***	***4***	***-***	***-***	***3***
It depends	2	-	2	1	1	-	2	-	-	1	1	1	1	1	1	2	-	-	2
	2	***-***	***3***	***2***	***4***	***-***	***3***	***-***	***-***	***3***	***2***	***2***	***3***	***1***	***3***	***3***	***-***	***-***	***2***
Don't know	3	1	2	2	-	1	2	1	1	-	2	-	1	2	1	-	1	2	3
	3	***2***	***3***	***3***	***-***	***4***	***3***	***2***	***3***	***-***	***4***	***-***	***3***	***3***	***3***	***-***	***14***	***7***	***3***
No response	2	1	1	-	1	1	-	2	1	1	-	-	-	1	1	-	-	-	2
	2	***2***	***2***	***-***	***4***	***4***	***-***	***5***	***3***	***3***	***-***	***-***	***-***	***1***	***3***	***-***	***-***	***-***	***2***

Key: Coun.=Council; F=Female; M=Male; Priv.=Private; Stud.=Student.

Selected Bibliography

Ashworth, A. (1986), 'Punishment and compensation: victims, offenders and the state', *Oxford Journal of Legal Studies*, 86.

—— (1992), 'The Criminal Justice Act 1991', in Munro, C. and Wasik, M. (eds.), *Sentencing, Judicial Discretion and Training*, Sweet and Maxwell.

—— (1993), 'Victim impact statements and sentencing', *Criminal Law Review*, 498.

—— (1995), *Sentencing and Criminal Justice*, Butterworths.

Aye Maung, N. (1995), 'Survey design and interpretation of the British Crime Survey', in Walker, M. (ed.), *Interpreting Crime Statistics*, Clarendon Press.

Baxter, J. and Koffman, L. (1985), *Police: The Constitution and the Community*, Professional Books.

Becker, H. (1973), *Outsiders*, Free Press, Macmillan.

Binney, V., Harkell, G. and Nixon, J. (1985), 'Refuges and housing for battered women', in Pahl, J. (ed.), *Private Violence and Public Policy*, Routledge.

Bottomley, A. K. and Coleman, C. (1981), *Understanding Crime Rates: Police and Public Roles in the Production of Official Statistics*, Saxon House.

Bottomley, K. and Pease, K. (1986), *Crime and Punishment: Interpreting the Data*, Open University Press.

Bottoms, A., Mawby, R., and Walker, M. (1987), 'A localised crime survey in contrasting areas of a city', *British Journal of Criminology*, 125.

Brogden, M., Jefferson, T. and Walklate, S. (1988), *Introducing Policework*, Unwin Hyman.

Bucke, T. (1995), *Policing and the Public: Findings from the 1994 British Crime Survey*, Research Findings No. 28, Home Office Research and Statistics Department.

Burrows, J. and Tarling, R. (1982), *Clearing Up Crime*, Home Office Research Study, HMSO.

Chambers, G. and Millar, A. (1983), *Investigating Sexual Assault*, HMSO.

Chapman, D. (1968), *Sociology and the Stereotype of the Criminal*, Tavistock.

Cohen, S. (ed.), (1971), *Images of Deviance*, Penguin.

Corbett, C. and Hobdell, K. (1988), 'Volunteer-based services to rape victims: some recent developments', in Maguire, M. and Pointing, J. (eds.), *Victims of Crime: A New Deal?*, Open University Press.

Crawford, A., Jones, T., Woodhouse, T. and Young, J. (1990), *Second Islington Crime Survey*, Middlesex Polytechnic.

Dyfed-Powys Police, (1994), *External Survey*, 1994, unpublished survey, prepared by its Research and Development Quality Support Department.

Eysenck, H. (1964), *Crime and Personality*, Paladin.

Farrell, G. (1992), 'Multiple victimisation: its extent and significance', *International Review of Victimology*, 85.

Farrell, G. and Pease, K. (1993), *Once Bitten, Twice Bitten: Repeat Victimisation and its Implications for Crime Prevention*, Crime Prevention Unit Paper, Home Office.

Farrington, D. and Gunn, J. (eds.), (1985), *Reactions to Crime: the Police, Courts and Prisons*, Wiley.

Fitzgerald, M. and Hale, C. (1996), *Ethnic Minorities Victimisation and Racial Harassment*, Home Office Research Study, HMSO.

Grace, S. (1995), *Policing Domestic Violence in the 1990s*, Home Office Research Study, HMSO.

Hall, R. (1985), *Ask Any Woman: A London Inquiry into Rape and Sexual Assault*, Falling Wall Press.

Harding, C. and Koffman, L. (1995), *Sentencing and the Penal System* (2nd edn.), Sweet and Maxwell.

Harris Research Centre (1987), *Crime in Newham*, London Borough of Newham.

Hart, H. L. A. (1968), *Punishment and Responsibility*, Clarendon Press.

Hirst, P. (1994), 'Rebirth of the parish constable', *Policing*, 196.

Holtom, C. and Raynor, P. (1988), 'Origins of victims support philosophy and practice', in Maguire, M. and Pointing, J. (eds.), *Victims of Crime: A New Deal?*, Open University Press.

Home Office (1964), *Compensation for Victims of Crimes of Violence*, Cmnd. 2323, HMSO.

—— (1990), *Victim's Charter: A Statement of the Rights of Victims of Crime*, HMSO.

—— (1994), *The General Household Survey 1993*, HMSO.

Hough, M. (1995), *Anxiety about Crime: Findings from the 1994 British Crime Survey*, Home Office Research Study, HMSO.

Hough, M. and Mayhew, P. (1983), *The British Crime Survey*, HMSO.

—— (1985), *Taking Account of Crime: Key Findings from the 1984 British Crime Survey*, Home Office Research Study, HMSO.

Hough, M. and Moxon, D. (1985), 'Dealing with offenders: popular opinion and the views of victims', *Howard Journal*, 160.

Jones, T., Maclean, B., and Young, J. (1986), *The Islington Crime Survey*, Gower.

Kelk, C., Koffman, L. and Silvis, J. (1995), 'Sentencing practice, policy and discretion', in Fennell, P. et al. (eds), *Criminal Justice in Europe*, Clarendon Press.

Kinsey, R. (1984), *The Merseyside Crime Survey, First Report*, Merseyside County Council.

—— (1985), *Survey of Merseyside Police Officers: First Report*, Merseyside County Council.

Kinsey, R., Lea, J. and Young, J. (1986), *Losing the Fight Against Crime*, Blackwell.

Lehnan, R. and Skogan, W. (eds.) (1981), *The National Crime Survey: Working Papers*, Vol. 1, U.S. Department of Justice.

Lloyd, S., Farrell, G. and Pease, K. (1994), *Preventing Repeated Domestic Violence: A Demonstration Project on Merseyside*, a Crime Prevention Unit Paper, Home Office.

Maguire, M. (1994), 'Crime Statistics, Patterns, and Trends: Changing Perceptions and their Implications', in Maguire, M. et al. (eds.), *Oxford Handbook of Criminology*, Clarendon Press.

Maguire, M. and Corbett, C. (1987), *The Effects of Crime and the Work of Victim Support Schemes*, Gower.

Maguire, M. and Pointing, J. (eds.), (1988), *Victims of Crime: A New Deal?*, Open University Press.

Mannheim, H. (1965), *Comparative Criminology*, Routledge.

Martin, J. P. (1962), *Offenders as Employees,* Macmillan.

Mawby, R. (1988), 'Victims' needs or victims' rights: alternative approaches to policy-making', in Maguire, M. and Pointing, J. (eds.), *Victims of Crime: A New Deal?*, Open University Press.

Mawby, R. and Walklate, S. (1994), *Critical Victimology*, Sage.

Maxfield, M. G. (1984), *Fear of Crime in England and Wales*, Home Office Research Study, HMSO.

Mayhew, P. (1995), 'Some methodological issues in victimisation surveys', in *Crime Victims Surveys in Australia*, Conference Proceedings, Brisbane Criminal Justice Commission.

Mayhew, P., Aye Maung, N. and Mirlees-Black, C. (1993), *The 1992 British Crime Survey*, HMSO.

Mayhew, P., Elliott, D., and Dowds, L. (1989), *The 1988 British Crime Survey*, Home Office Research Study, HMSO.

Mayhew, P. and Hough, M. (1988), 'The British Crime Survey: origins and impact', in Maguire, M. and Pointing, J. (eds.), *Victims of Crime: A New Deal?*, Open University Press.

Mayhew, P., Mirlees-Black, C. and Aye Maung, N. (1994), *Trends in Crime: Findings from the 1994 British Crime Survey*, Research Findings No. 14, Home Office Research and Statistics Department.

McCabe, S. and Sutcliffe, F. (1978), *Defining Crime: A Study of Police Decisions*, Oxford University Centre for Criminological Research.

Miers, D. (1978), *Responses to Victimisation*, Professional Books.

—— (1992), 'The responsibilities and the rights of victims of crime', *Modern Law Review*, 483.

Mirlees-Black, C. and Ross, A. (1995), *Crime Against Retail Premises in 1993*, Research Findings No. 26, Home Office Research and Statistics Department.

—— (1995), *Crime Against Manufacturing Premises in 1993*, Research Findings No. 27, Home Office Research and Statistics Department.

Morgan, J. et al., 'Protection of and compensation for victims of crime', in Fennell, P. et al. (eds.), *Criminal Justice In Europe*, Clarendon Press.

Morgan, J. and Zedner, L. (1992), *Child Victims: Crime, Impact and Criminal Justice*, Clarendon Press.

Moxon, D., Corkery, J. M., and Hedderman, C. (1992), *Development in the Use of Compensation Orders in Magistrates' Courts since October 1988*, HMSO.

Newburn, T. (1988), *The Use and Enforcement of Compensation Orders in Magistrates' Courts*, Home Office Research Study, HMSO.

—— (1989) *The Settlement of Claims at the Criminal Injuries Compensation Board*, Home Office Research Study, HMSO.

Newburn, T. and Merry, S. (1990), *Keeping in Touch: Police–Victim Communication in Two Areas*, Home Office Research Study, HMSO.

Osborn, D. et al. (1992), 'Area characteristics and regional variates as determinants of area property crime levels', *Journal of Quantitative Criminology*, 265

Pease, K. (1988), *Judgement of Crime Seriousness: Evidence from the 1984 British Crime Survey*, Home Office Research and Planning Unit Paper, HMSO.

Pease, K. (1993), 'Individual and community influences on victimisation and their implications for crime prevention', in Farrington, D. et al. (eds.), *Integrating Individual and Ecological Aspects of Crime*, BRÅ-report.

—— (1994), 'Cross-national imprisonment rates', *British Journal of Criminology*, 116.

Pease, K. and Hukkila, K. (eds.), (1990), *Criminal Justice Systems in Europe and North America*, HEUNI.

Pizzey, E. (1974), *Scream Quietly or the Neighbours Will Hear*, Penguin.

Plotnikoff, J. and Woolfson, R. (1995), *Prosecuting Child Abuse*, Blackstone.

Polvi, N. (1991), 'The time course of repeat burglary victimisation', *British Journal of Criminology*, 411.

Raine, J. and Smith, R. (1991), *The Victim/Witness in Court Project: Report of the Research Programme*, Victim Support.

Ralphs, Lady (1988), *The Victim in Court: Report of the Working Party*, NAVSS.

Ramsay, M. and Percy, A. (1996), *Drug Misuse Declared: Results of the 1994 British Crime Survey*, Home Office Research Study, HMSO.

Reiner, R. (1992), *The Politics of the Police* (2nd edn.), Wheatsheaf.

Rock, P. (1990), *Helping Victims of Crime*, Clarendon Press.

Rock, P. and McIntosh M. (eds.), (1974), *Deviance and Social Control*, Tavistock.

Ross, A. (1975), *On Guilt, Responsibility and Punishment*, Stevens.

Royal Commission on Criminal Justice (1993), *Report*, Cm. 2263, HMSO.

Rutherford, A. (1984), *Prisons and the Process of Justice*, Heinemann.

Schaaf, R. (1986), 'New international instruments in crime prevention and criminal justice', *International Journal of Legal Information*, 176.

Shapland, J. and Vagg, J. (1988), *Policing By the Public*, Routledge.

Shapland, J., Willmore, J. and Duff, P. (1985), *Victims in the Criminal Justice System*, Gower.

Sim, J., Scraton, P. and Gordon, P. (1987), 'Introduction: crime, the state and critical analysis', in Scraton, P. (ed.), *Law, Order and the Authoritarian State*, Open University Press.

Skogan, W. G. (1990), *The Police and the Public in England and Wales: A British Crime Survey Report*, Home Office Research Study, HMSO.

Skogan, W.G. (1994), *Contacts Between Police and Public: findings from the 1992 British Crime Survey*, Home Office Research Study, HMSO.

Smith, D. and Gray, J. (1985), *Police and People in London*, Policy Studies Institute.

Sparks, R. (1981), 'Multiple victimisation: evidence, theory and future research', *Journal of Criminal Law and Criminology*, 762.

Sparks, R., Genn, H., and Dodd, D. (1977), *Surveying Victims*, Wiley.

Stanko, E. (1988), 'Hidden violence against women', in Maguire, M. and Pointing, J. (eds.), *Victims of Crime: A New Deal?*, Open University Press.

Sutherland, E. H. (1949), *White Collar Crime*, Holt Rinehart and Winston.

T. Anna., (1988), 'Feminist responses to sexual abuse: the work of the Birmingham Rape Crisis Centre', in Maguire, M. and Pointing, J. (eds.), *Victims of Crime: A New Deal?*, Open University Press.

Temkin, J. (1987), *Rape and the Legal Process*, Sweet and Maxwell.

Van Dijk, J. (1988), 'Ideological trends within the victims movement: an international perspective' in Maguire, M. and Pointing, J. (eds.), *Victims of Crime: A New Deal?*, Open University Press.

Van Dijk, J. and Mayhew, P. (1993), *Criminal Victimisation in the Industrialised World: Key Findings from the 1989 and 1992 International Crime Survey*, Directorate of Crime Prevention, Ministry of Justice, The Hague.

Wasik, M. and Taylor, R. (1994), *Criminal Justice Act 1991* (2nd edn.), Blackstone.

Whitaker, C. and Bastian, L. (1991), *Teenager Victims: A National Crime Survey Report*, US Department of Justice, Washington DC.

Wiles, P. (1971), 'Criminal statistics and sociological explanations of crime', in Carson, W. G. and Wiles, P. (eds.), *The Sociology of Crime and Delinquency in Britain*, Martin Robertson.

Young, J. (1988), 'Risk of crime and fear of crime: a realist critique of survey-based assumptions', in Maguire, M. and Pointing, J. (eds.), *Victims of Crime: A New Deal?*, Open University Press.

Zedner, L. (1994), 'Victims', in Maguire, M., et al. (eds.), *Oxford Handbook of Criminology*, Clarendon Press.

Index